A Beginner's Guide to Descartes's *Meditations*

For Gran, and in loving memory of Gramps,
who have never failed in their love and support, or in the patient hope
that one day I might earn a living – or even get married.

A Beginner's Guide to Descartes's *Meditations*

Gareth Southwell

BLACKWELL PUBLISHING
350 Main Street, Malden, MA 02148-5020, USA
9600 Garsington Road, Oxford OX4 2DQ, UK
550 Swanston Street, Carlton, Victoria 3053, Australia

First published 2008 by Blackwell Publishing Ltd

1 2008

Library of Congress Cataloging-in-Publication Data

Southwell, Gareth.
A beginner's guide to Descartes's Meditations / Gareth Southwell.
p. cm.
Includes bibliographical references and index.
ISBN 978-1-4051-5854-1 (hardcover : alk. paper) – ISBN 978-1-4051-5855-8 (pbk.: alk. paper) 1. Descartes, René, 1596–1650. Meditationes de prima philosophia. 2. First philosophy. 3. God–Proof, Ontological. I. Title.

B1854.S68 2008
194–dc22

2007023100

A catalogue record for this title is available from the British Library.

Set in 10 on 12.5 pt Minion
by SNP Best-set Typesetter Ltd., Hong Kong

For further information on
Blackwell Publishing, visit our website at
www.blackwellpublishing.com

Contents

List of Illustrations and Tables

Acknowledgements

Firstly, I must thank everyone who read the manuscript and gave me valuable feedback at its various stages of development. Of the friends and family who took the time to read it, honourable mentions go to Ali Morrison, Phill Burton, Mike Kirwan, and Gwen Wright (the Common-Mother-in-Law). A more academically informed (though still slightly partisan) eye was cast over it by my good friend Dr Mark Matthews, and all his suggestions to do with punctuation, referencing, and style have been roundly and foolishly ignored!

Many teaching acquaintances were also kind enough to take the time to give me their informed opinions. This contribution was especially valuable, and at a time when the project was in the balance, this positive feedback was a key factor in swaying it. So, my sincere thanks and gratitude must go to George McWilliams, Gavin Palmer, Jules Bennett, Paul Britton, Judith Gardom, Katharine Watson, and Rob Snelling and his students. Other academic opinions were also forthcoming from some early anonymous reviewers, and my thanks to them for their insightful and at times painstaking comments. I hope that they will see the improvement in this final published version.

Thanks must also go to those of my ex-students who took time to turn their minds to all things Cartesian (*again*), and to give me their opinions. Of these, special thanks must go to Amanda Gwynne, who took time off from her undergraduate workload (such a difficulty for a student) to supply her thoughts on the matter. For those of them who were too busy to get back to me in time, may they suffer the special torments particular to that circle of hell reserved for those who do not provide feedback on guides to Descartes in manuscript. As a punishment, I shall ensure that they read my guide to Nietzsche.

In terms of financial support, I was lucky enough to receive a grant from the Authors' Foundation, which was a welcome contribution to the costs of maintaining my bohemian lifestyle (i.e. Marmite and fresh ground coffee) – for which, my thanks.

I must of course thank Nick Bellorini, the commissioning editor for philosophy at Blackwell, who was perspicacious enough to see past the rough edges and the inappropriate humour to a work worthy of publication (though I think I almost persuaded him to keep some of the jokes in . . .). I trust he will accept Italy winning the World Cup as part payment for this debt of gratitude.

Thanks to Julian Baggini and Jeremy Stangroom of *The Philosophers' Magazine*, for my first big break in caricature (I still think 'Philosophers Top Trumps' is a good idea!).

Please accept my apologies if you do not find your name here: I am sometimes a bear of very little brain.

My love and gratitude must go to my family for their general support: to Jo, for help with the proofreading and indexing, but primarily for taking the kids out of my way; and to Eli and Tes (the kids), for being out of the way (words cannot express).

Lastly, my belated thanks go out to the late Dick Beardsmore (perhaps the first victim of my inappropriate humour – 'the jokes don't add much') and, sadly, the also recently deceased Dewi Phillips, both of whom I was lucky enough to have as teachers when I was an undergraduate at Swansea. In their different ways, both instilled in me their passion for philosophy, which they communicated with humour and lack of pretension. Thank you.

Introduction

The seventeenth-century French philosopher René Descartes is considered by many to be the founding father of modern philosophy. However, just as it has been said that the European philosophical tradition can best be thought of as 'a series of footnotes to Plato',[1] so it may be argued that the importance of Descartes lies more in the problems he identified and tried to answer, than in the success of the actual solutions which he proposed. Many philosophy courses at all levels will therefore at some point involve, to greater or lesser degree, reference to Descartes's philosophy. So, wherever scepticism is discussed, or the issue of how we may be certain about our knowledge is addressed, where the nature of the mind is considered, or the possible existence of the soul is debated, Descartes is likely at some point to put in an appearance.

However, Descartes is also important in other respects. Firstly, he is in many ways representative of an age. The seventeenth century marked a turning point in Western society as it moved away from tradition and dogma (represented by the Catholic Church) towards scientific inquiry. Descartes's concerns are thus also those of science, of a man who is looking to establish how we can find things out for ourselves instead of merely relying on the dictates of authority – whether those of the state or of religion. That said, Descartes was actually a complex individual who, to a modern eye, appears to be riven with contradictions: as a man of science he was concerned with the advancement of knowledge by solely rational means;[2] however, as a religious believer, he was also keen to find arguments in support of religious doctrine and thereby convince non-believers of its truth.[3] This combination of scientific zeal and religious faith is perhaps difficult for the majority of modern people to empathize with. However, to others, this aspect of Descartes's philosophy will no doubt be a point of interest in itself.

For those interested in Descartes's philosophy in general, the *Meditations* provides an ideal introduction to his thought in that it contains pretty much all of his main philosophical opinions. The purpose of this book is therefore to provide help to those studying the *Meditations* (at whatever level), those who encounter Descartes as part of a philosophy course, those who touch upon his philosophy as part of other studies, and finally, those who merely have a general interest in the man and his ideas. So, whether you are a philosophy student or not, this book is, I hope, written in a way that does not require any specialist knowledge or acquaintance with philosophy, while at the same time avoiding being in any way simplistic or patronizing.

Regarding the structure of the book, the first chapter deals with all the background needed to gain an understanding of the context of Descartes's ideas. This first chapter is not actually essential to a clear understanding of Descartes's philosophy, but it will help to show how Descartes's ideas fit into their historical context (for those who are interested). The second chapter provides a non-critical, step-by-step overview of the *Meditations* itself, and my main purpose here is to present the central ideas and concerns in as clear a way as possible, while also trying to maintain the narrative flow of Descartes's text. The third and final chapter provides a critical analysis of Descartes and his philosophy through the topics it touches upon. Here, I have tried to give an overview of the types of criticism that Descartes's ideas have received, as well as showing how these concerns relate to various topics within philosophy.

I have tried to keep notes to a minimum, but where they exist, they are mostly for those who wish to follow up any references, quotations, or directions to further reading that I make (for this reason, I have placed them at the end of the book). Sometimes, also, these notes contain information which would interrupt the flow of the writing, or relate to a topic that I do not cover because, however interesting, it is not directly relevant.

In Appendix A I have provided an overview of the *Meditations* itself, briefly detailing the arguments as they occur. In Appendix B, there is a summary of certain parts of Descartes's published correspondence with his contemporaries (the *Objections and Replies*), where those who wish to delve more deeply into the text will find useful material. Following this, there is a glossary where the reader can find simple definitions of certain terms used in the book.

There is a bibliography at the end for those who want to delve into the subject more deeply through further reading. I have grouped the works listed under headings with a few lines of description so that the undergraduate, A-Level student, student from another discipline, or general reader, can hunt down the book that would best suit his or her needs.

Finally, I am responsible for the website www.philosophyonline.co.uk, where can be found notes relating to a number of areas of philosophy (including Descartes). In producing this guide it has been my intention to try to keep the information which is freely available on the site distinct from the published material. So, for instance, on the site the eager student will find a fully annotated online edition of the *Meditations*, study questions, a guide to exam technique, and other study-related material which would only detract from the more general purpose of this text. On a small number of occasions the same material (certain tables and summaries) can be found in both places. However, this is a very infrequent occurrence, and in general the two resources are independent and complementary to one another.

If you have any comments, questions, suggestions, wish to report any spelling mistakes, typos, factual inaccuracies, or undertake any of the other wonderful things that email is good for, then you can contact me by using the form on the website.

I hope you enjoy the book.

Gareth Southwell

Chapter 1

Background

Life of Descartes[1]

René Descartes was born on 31 March 1596 in the small town of La Haye in the Touraine region of France (which, for this reason, was renamed

René Descartes (1596-1650)

La Haye-Descartes in 1802, and subsequently, in 1967, simply *Descartes*). His mother having died when he was only one year old, he lived from that time on with his elder brother and sister in the house of his maternal grandmother. Between the ages of ten and eighteen he attended the Jesuit College of La Flèche at Anjou (he remained a devout Catholic throughout his life), and around 1614–15 he moved to a house just outside Paris, where he chose to live alone. It is while living here that he seems to have suffered a nervous breakdown. The next year he attended the University of Poitiers, where he studied not philosophy, but civil and canon law, and also possibly a little medicine.

At the age of twenty-two, keen to get some experience of the world, he began to travel. In 1618 he enlisted in the Dutch army as a gentleman soldier, where he first met Isaac Beeckman, a Dutch philosopher and scientist, who rekindled Descartes's interest in such matters.

On his return to France in 1619, Descartes seems to have undergone some sort of mystical experience which was to change his life. The revelation took the form of three consecutive dreams, and is understood to have left Descartes with the conviction that the universe was divinely designed and ordered on rational principles. This revelation, combining as it does aspects of both science and religion, is perhaps central to understanding Descartes and his outlook on life – and especially his purpose in writing the *Meditations*.

Over the next ten years, Descartes travelled to various parts of Europe, ranging between the Netherlands, Italy, and France, but never settling in one place for too long. During this time, he had contact with various scholars, scientists, and philosophers, and through conversation, debate, and correspondence, began to formalize his own views more clearly. In 1628, however, he moved to the Netherlands, where he lived – albeit in different places – for the next twenty years.

In 1635, a daughter, Francine, was born to Hélène, a serving maid at the house where he had been staying in Amsterdam. However, while Descartes seems to have taken a growing interest in the child, and to have contributed financially to the welfare of both mother and daughter, the relationship with Hélène seems to have been a short-lived thing. Tragically, however, his relationship with his daughter was also not destined to last very long, and she died of a fever at the age of five.

During this time, Descartes's reputation had been steadily growing. His *Rules for the Direction of the Mind* had been completed in 1628, but was not to be published until after his death. Another work, his projected revision of current scientific knowledge, *De Mundo*, was almost ready for publication when, in 1633, Descartes heard of the fate of Galileo (with whom his work shared a Copernican – therefore heretical – view of the solar system), so he withheld publication. Slowly, however, over the next few years, he tentatively released those parts of this material which he considered would not offend the Church, until in 1637 he released *A Discourse on Method*, which collected much of the already published material in one volume, and contained his theories on light, meteors, and some discoveries in analytic geometry. The volume also contained the first account of his scientific and philosophical method, and it is this introductory part which is now most famous. In 1641, he reworked these philosophical ideas into the first text of the *Meditations on the First Philosophy*, which was originally published in Latin. It was this text which was to generate the most controversy amongst philosophers, theologians, and scholars (both for and against), and during most of the 1640s Descartes's time was taken up with defending and expanding upon the philosophical ideas presented there. The *Principles of Philosophy* followed in 1644, and restated the main ideas of the *Meditations*, together with certain of Descartes's theories concerning the structure of the universe and the nature of the soul. The final work to be published during his lifetime, *The Passions of the Soul*, was Descartes's attempt to put ethics on a scientific footing, and it appeared in 1649.

In the last year of his life he moved to Stockholm to tutor Queen Christina of Sweden. Apparently, the Queen – a habitual early riser – would arrange meetings with Descartes at 5 a.m. in a large, poorly heated, and draughty room. Little wonder, then, that he duly caught the cold which eventually led to his death, from pneumonia, on 11 February 1650, shortly before his fifty-fourth birthday.

The Cultural Context

No ideas exist in isolation from their historical context, and the further away the ideas are from the present day, the more need there is to understand the times which gave birth to them. In Descartes's case, the time is the seventeenth century, and the place is western Europe. However, while it is true that Descartes was a French philosopher, many philosophers and scholars of the time chose to write in Latin, thus providing a common academic language for thinkers from most European countries.[2]

As I have already mentioned in the Introduction, this period marked a turning point in the history of ideas. It was a time when the power of the Catholic Church was still great, but when old ideas were being challenged through the growth of scientific inquiry. When Galileo pledged his support for the Polish astronomer Copernicus's idea that the Sun was the centre of the universe in a work published in 1632,[3] he was soon after imprisoned by the Inquisition.[4] This event had a great effect on Descartes, and (as noted above) he put off publishing his philosophical work while he thought out the best way to introduce his ideas without incurring the wrath of the Church (when he finally did publish his *Discourse and Essays* some years later, it was anonymously).[5]

Philosophically, Descartes's approach can be contrasted with the traditional approach of the time, which we now refer to as *scholasticism*. Descartes sometimes refers in his writing to the 'philosophy of the schools' or 'schoolmen'. By this, he means the philosophical tradition which had become established in such *schools* or early universities as existed by the middle of the thirteenth century in cities all over Europe (the leading two existed in Paris and Oxford).[6]

The activities of these schools were based largely on the study of the works of the Greek philosopher Aristotle (384–322 BC) and the writings of his commentators. This led to a very formal, strict, and narrow focus almost solely on Aristotle's works and method, resulting in a tight union between Aristotelian philosophy and Christian doctrine (or rather, the Catholic Church's interpretation of the teachings of the Bible). As you may imagine, this environment was not really very conducive to the development of scientific method or free thinking, and the power of the Church ensured that any philosopher with unconventional views could be branded a religious heretic and face imprisonment, torture, or even death (which is one of the reasons why Descartes dedicates the *Meditations* to the Doctors of Theology in Paris!).[7]

To give you an idea of the sort of problems the early scientists faced in this period, consider the theory of gravity. Now, Aristotle's system predicts that any two objects falling to the ground will differ in their speed according to their weight. So, a heavier object will fall faster than a lighter one. This is because, according to Aristotle, every object will seek its 'natural place' in the universe, and heavy objects – because of their weight – will do so faster than light ones. However, in a famous experiment, the Italian philosopher and scientist, Galileo Galilei (1564–1642), tried to show how this was wrong. He is said to have taken a cannon ball and a small musket ball,[8] and, in front of a crowd of witnesses, to have dropped them both off the famous Leaning Tower in Pisa, Italy. However, rather than arriving at the ground at different times – as Aristotle would have predicted – the balls seemed to land at more or less the same time. The only factor which alters the rate at which objects fall, Galileo concluded, is air resistance. Therefore, the more surface area a thing has, the more the air will slow it down – hence, things with a smaller surface area, or aerodynamic things (which are designed to have little air resistance – such as arrows and aeroplanes) fly faster through the air.[9]

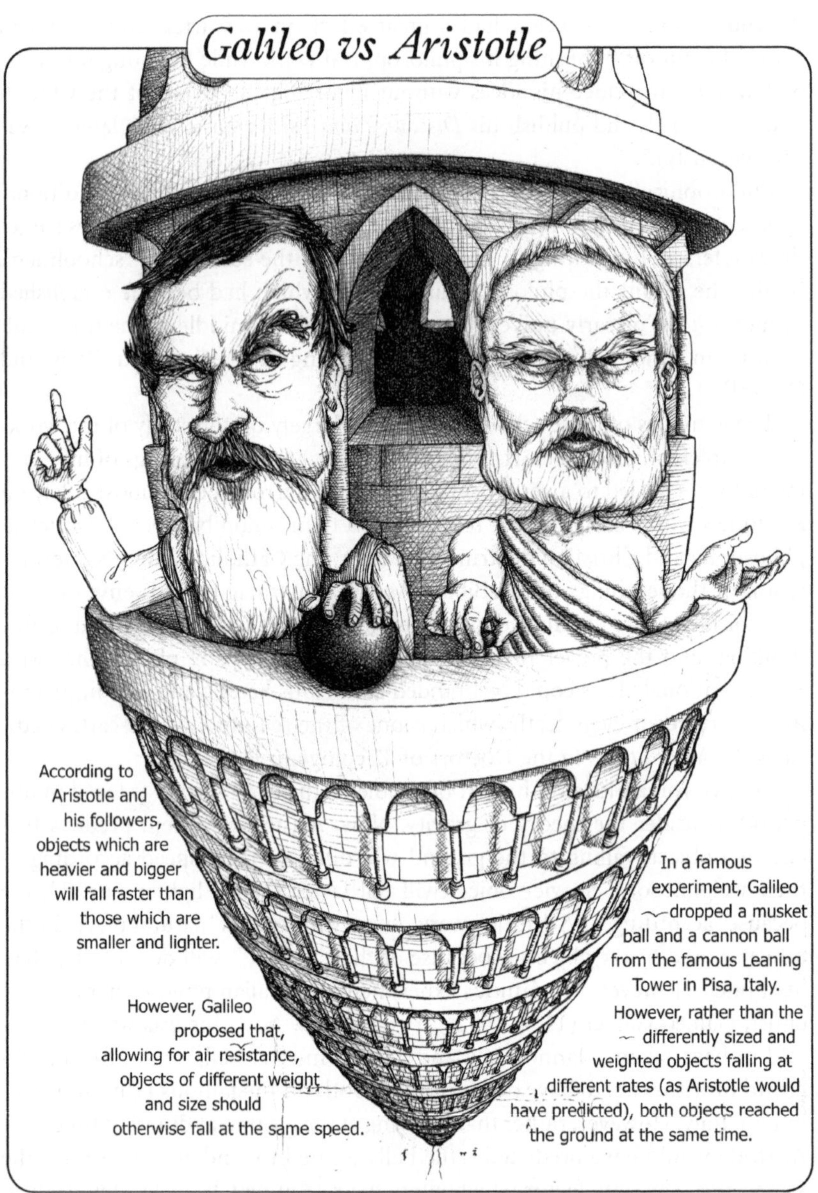
Galileo vs Aristotle
According to Aristotle and his followers, objects which are heavier and bigger will fall faster than those which are smaller and lighter.
However, Galileo proposed that, allowing for air resistance, objects of different weight and size should otherwise fall at the same speed.
In a famous experiment, Galileo dropped a musket ball and a cannon ball from the famous Leaning Tower in Pisa, Italy. However, rather than the differently sized and weighted objects falling at different rates (as Aristotle would have predicted), both objects reached the ground at the same time.

The Purpose of the Meditations

The *Meditations*, or to give it its fuller title, *Meditations on the First Philosophy*, was published in Latin in 1641. In many ways, it is a restatement and refinement of ideas which Descartes had already developed in his earlier work, the *Discourse on Method*, but expressed at greater length and in a narrative format. The book contains six Meditations, each of which is supposed to take place on a different day. The reader is thus led, step by step, along with Descartes on his journey towards – hopefully – the same conclusions as the author.

The main theme which propels the narrative of the *Meditations* is the search for certainty. Cleverly, Descartes presents the text as if it is an answer to the *theological* sceptics and unbelievers who have questioned such things as whether there is a God, and whether the soul exists (and is immortal). However, in doing this, he also sets out his method for finding truth *in the sciences*. In this way, Descartes is also hoping to release the hold that Church dogma and the followers of Aristotle, and scholastic philosophy in general, have had over the development of philosophy and science, and at the same time to establish a way in which science, philosophy, and religion can coexist in harmony.

The problem, then, for both scientists and philosophers, was that the dogma of the Church and the doctrines of Aristotle were thought together to represent the last word on the nature of reality. Scientific experiment, therefore, was not so much unthought-of, but rather not thought *necessary*, since all that we may wish to know can be worked out from consideration of the so-called *first principles* that govern reality (such as formed the basis of Aristotle's ideas regarding falling bodies). However, many of these first principles were themselves based on speculation, and under certain circumstances (such as Galileo's experiment from the tower in Pisa), could in fact be seen to be wrong. Thus Descartes saw his first task as being to utilize certain sceptical arguments in order to expose these false assumptions, and ultimately arrive at the *true* first principles.

The method Descartes employs in the *Meditations* to achieve this has become known as his 'method of doubt'. Thus he begins not by stating things which he thinks are true and building upon them, but by asking the simple question, 'Is there any one thing of which we can be absolutely certain?' In tackling the problem in this way, Descartes attempts to find the one thing beyond all doubt upon which we can build our knowledge – the *very first* principle, so to speak.

Chapter 2

Explanation and Summary of Main Arguments

Introduction

This chapter is intended to provide a clear and easy-to-understand overview of the *Meditations*, argument by argument. I think that it is important to get a feeling for the *Meditations* as almost a type of story (it might be called, 'How I Overcame Doubt and Uncertainty, Found the One Indubitable Truth, and Guaranteed Knowledge of the External World' by René Descartes – or something catchy like that). Just as stories have a narrative or sense of logical progression and connection, so the *Meditations* can be viewed as a sort of journey. This may be summarized – very broadly – as follows:

1. Beginning with his everyday opinions, the author comes to realize that many of them are based on false assumptions or unwarranted assertions.
2. Through rigorous questioning and use of sceptical argument the author finds that he is able to doubt everything he once thought that he was certain of – even his own existence.
3. However, the darkest hour being before the dawn, it suddenly occurs to Descartes that he can be absolutely sure of at least one thing: while he thinks, he must also exist (the famous *Cogito ergo sum*: 'I think, therefore I am').
4. From here, the traveller is able to light his way back along the still difficult way home.
5. Arriving back, things are not what they were. He is changed from his journey, yet now possesses the key knowledge that allows him to understand the world and himself better.

The six Meditations appear to take place on six separate days. So, in the course of the text we sometimes come across phrases like 'The Meditation of yesterday . . .'[1] or '. . . in the same way that I yesterday examined the idea . . .'.[2] This gives the impression of a journal or diary, and we are encouraged by Descartes to follow him in his thoughts on a parallel journey of our own:

> I would advise none to read this work, unless such as are able and willing to meditate with me in earnest, to detach their minds from commerce with the senses, and likewise to deliver themselves from all prejudice[3]

The *Meditations* therefore has a personal tone which is rarely found in philosophy – one of the things which possibly accounts for its lasting appeal. In summarizing and commenting on the arguments, therefore, I have tried to retain this sense of narrative progression and shared journey. For convenience's sake, however, I have also provided a simplified overview of the arguments in table form (this can be found in Appendix A).

Finally, I would not wish the summary of the arguments presented below to substitute for an actual reading of the *Meditations* itself. Firstly, the notes are meant to aid understanding and not merely to paraphrase Descartes. So, in doing this, I have added some of my own illustrations and examples. Thus, anyone studying Descartes needs to know which bits actually come from Descartes, and which from me (and I'll never tell!). Secondly, for any serious student, there are complex points and additional detail that I could not or would not wish to render in a summary. This extra information is vital for a serious study of Descartes and is key to any discussion or disagreement about 'what he is really getting at'. Lastly, reading the *Meditations* is, once you get past the sometimes long-winded prose, a genuine enjoyment. I won't say, 'Or your money back!', since there is no accounting for taste (and I don't have much money). However, reading the text first hand can give you a better idea of what Descartes was trying to achieve and thus help develop a sympathetic reading of the text – and not just a caricature formed from secondary reading or discussion. However, please bear in mind that while I do not pass judgement on the arguments in summarizing them, that is not to say that I *agree* with them. On the other hand, while I critically examine those same arguments in Chapter 3, it is also not necessarily true that I *disagree* with them. Ultimately, in a guide of this sort my personal opinions do not matter, and my main purpose is to help you start to think about these issues for yourself in an informed way. So, while it is almost impossible to be completely impartial, I have made every effort to be so.

Meditation I: About the Things We May Doubt

Introduction

We've all had the thought. You're sitting there in your pyjamas, wondering if you should have had that last cup of coffee so late in the evening, when it strikes you: how can I be certain that I know anything? How do I know that I am not mistaken about everything? That life is not a dream, that everyone I spoke to today wasn't in fact a robot, and that there isn't an evil demon whose sole enjoyment in life comes from making me believe a whole lot of nonsense? (Well, maybe not everyone – perhaps, in fact, only philosophers.)

We may credit Descartes with being one of the first philosophers to entertain these thoughts in a sober-headed, 'I'm going to get to the bottom of this', sort of way. Realizing the importance of this issue, and also that the problem isn't just going to go away, he sets about analysing his opinions, beliefs, and attitudes with a view to seeing how certain they are. In fact, this is no little undertaking, for Descartes is not just setting out to rid himself of false opinions, but furthermore to reject everything which is in the least bit uncertain. He is not going to do this belief by belief, however, but rather – as he says – by 'an assault first on the principles on which all my former opinions were based'.[4] So, even at this early stage, Descartes is concerned with finding out *why* his beliefs are uncertain, and declares himself determined 'to begin afresh from the foundations'.[5] But what do these foundations consist of?

Admittedly, not all of us are concerned with the necessity of establishing 'something firm and constant in the sciences'.[6] However, inasmuch as we can follow Descartes's journey, we are all concerned with personal knowledge and the need to be certain about things. Again, I think this is one of the most appealing things about the *Meditations* in that it presents the problem of knowledge in terms of personal experience. Admittedly, the discussion can get quite surreal at certain points of Descartes's narrative (as it can in any philosophical discussion), but the starting point at least is one that we can practically engage with immediately. This is also, I think, why certain types of sceptical argument remain popular themes in film and literature, because they start with what is familiar to us (our immediate experience of the world).[7]

The Argument from Illusion

The first big conclusion that Descartes arrives at concerns the actual source of his information about the world:

> Everything I have accepted up to now as being absolutely true and assured, I have learned from or through the senses.[8]

This is not to say that Descartes believes that the only way we receive our ideas is through our senses – this would make him an *empiricist* (and, in fact, he is a *rationalist* – a distinction which I will go into later[9]). What he is saying is merely that human beings are mostly reliant on the impressions that we receive through our senses in order to make judgements, gather information, establish proof, etc. However, he also notes that our senses can mislead us. This is, in fact, quite an old idea in philosophical circles, having been introduced (or at least popularized) by Plato. Both these philosophers believed that the senses could, on occasion, provide us with wrong information and that, as a result, we should not place total trust in them. Furthermore, they were both rationalists and had a similar suggestion as to how we might achieve true knowledge (but this is skipping ahead somewhat – let's get back to the subject of the senses).

The argument that the senses mislead us and cannot be trusted is commonly known as the *argument from illusion*. In other words, it is the view that what we see, hear, feel, etc., may be an illusory representation of what really exists. A famous example often used to illustrate this supposed illusion is the fact that when a straight stick is half submerged in water it appears bent. Other examples include the occurrence of mirages (where, for example, the heat of a desert, or a hot road, may make it appear that there is a stretch of water up ahead, when in fact there is not), optical illusions (such as lines of equal length appearing unequal under certain conditions), and the appearance of light from stars which, because of the time taken for the light to reach us, are in fact no longer there (obviously, this last example would have been unknown to Descartes since the finite speed of light was yet to be discovered – though it still illustrates an aspect of the same problem that would have concerned Descartes).

The Mirage

Descartes's conclusion from all this is that, because the senses have once deceived us, we should not trust them at all. This, he admits, may seem to some to be an extreme conclusion, for aren't there ordinary perceptions that we have everyday that are completely trustworthy – such as the perception that I am sitting here now, reading this sentence? This sort of perception does not take place under unusual situations (such as the mirage), or involve distant objects (such as the stars), so why can't we trust it?

The Argument from Dreaming

It is at this point that Descartes introduces his second major sceptical argument: the *argument from dreaming*. Have we not all, he argues, at one time or another, *dreamt* that we were awake, or sitting in a chair reading? Well, perhaps not all of us – or even most of us. Perhaps, once again, only philosophers. However, his argument remains a powerful one: most of us would admit, even if we have not directly experienced it ourselves, that it is *possible* to dream that we are awake – and furthermore, *not to know it*!

The argument from dreaming is peculiarly powerful, then, for anything to which we may lay claim as proof that we are not dreaming may in fact form part of the dream itself. 'But what if I pinch myself?', you might say, 'That feels real. Therefore, I cannot be dreaming.' But when dreaming, the most fantastic things may happen and you may still think that they are real. How, then, can you be sure that the same thing is not happening now? In other words, your belief about what is real is related to your ability to be convinced of the fact, and if we are more easily convinced of things when we are dreaming, then *anything* could seem real to our dreaming self.

Dismayed with the powerful hold that the dreaming argument seems to have over him, Descartes looks for some consolation in the nature of dreaming itself. This he finds in the fact that, even if the images he is presented with in the course of his life are all false, and part only of some dream or grand illusion, *some* of the parts of which they are made up must at least have some reality. In other words, the dream images of individual objects – such as ships, people, animals, books, etc. – may not actually exist, but in considering them we can see that they involve more general ideas, such as shape (e.g. the roundness of an apple) and number (how many apples there are). So, while apples themselves may not exist, the principles of mathematics and geometry which the *idea* of apples involves may still apply, since such principles do not rely on the existence of anything for their truth. In other words, even if 'round things' do not exist, the idea of 'roundness' does. This is an important point for Descartes in that it allows him to establish a distinction between 'sciences which have for their end the consideration of composite objects [i.e. things made up of many parts]' – such as physics, astronomy, medicine – and sciences which 'regard merely the simplest and most general objects' – such as mathematics and geometry. Since the latter are not affected by the existence or non-existence of apples (but merely concern such ideas as 'roundness'), we cannot be mistaken about the truths which those studies involve (such as the truth of the equation that the circumference of a circle is equal to twice *pi* times its radius – or '2πr').

> For whether I am awake or sleeping, two and three added together always make five, and a square never has more than four sides; and it does not seem possible that truths so apparent can be suspected of any falsity or uncertainty.[10]

This idea will be important again later in the *Meditations* when Descartes is looking for a means of establishing just *which* ideas are most trustworthy and why. However, for now, it is important just to notice that, for Descartes, the ideas which have *least* connection with the senses are valued *most.*

The Evil Demon/Argument from Deception (Part One)

The final sceptical argument which Descartes entertains in the first Meditation goes furthest of all. Having already considered that the senses may be faulty, or that he may be dreaming, he now goes on to consider whether it might not be possible that he is even mistaken about the things which he has so far considered most certain – such as that the world exists, or that 2 + 2 = 4. Maybe, he reasons, it is possible for an all-powerful being to make it so that he is deceived even in regard to these apparent certainties. However, since God is by nature good, it seems unlikely that he should create human beings so that they may be systematically deceived regarding such beliefs *all* of the time. Still, this might not be beyond the capabilities of an all-powerful, supernatural being with evil intentions. Hence, the important question becomes, 'Who is responsible for my existence?' On the one hand, if his creator has good intentions, then the likelihood of our being constantly in error becomes less (for it would be against the nature of such a good being to create us so as never to know the truth regarding anything). On the other hand, if humans have been created by an evil demon of some sort, then the trustworthiness of these perceived truths is undermined (for such a being might be malicious enough to create us so as to be constantly mistaken).

This type of argument is known as the *argument from deception* and common examples of it can be found in many guises. For example, the idea that we are deliberately deceived by malevolent beings is a plot device of the *Matrix* films. For those of you who have been living in a remote cave in the Himalayas for the last ten years and aren't familiar with the plot, it revolves around the main character, Neo, who discovers that the world which he had up until now thought was 'real' is in fact a computer generated 'virtual reality'. In philosophy, this is similar to what is known as the *brains in vats* scenario, where it is imagined that what we think of as *reality* is no more than a series of electrical impulses fed to our disembodied brains as they sit in the laboratory of some deranged scientist. Other examples of deception can be found, of course, but the main theme is usually that we are deliberately deceived on just such a grand scale as Descartes imagines.[11] Since it is, in a way, the most extreme and powerful form of scepticism, Descartes will return to this argument again later on. However, for now, he is content to introduce the type of doubt that it represents and to argue that, combined with the previous two arguments – those from illusion and dreaming – there is a strong case for doubting the basis of *all* of our knowledge, and therefore a correspondingly strong need to find a way of guaranteeing it.

It should however be noted at this point that Descartes's deception argument differs from the brains in vats scenario in one important respect: Descartes is not asking, here, 'Am I merely the brain?' for, since the brain is a physical thing, and he can only presume at this point the existence of the physical world through his mental perceptions, this would be to assume the existence of something physical. What he *is* asking, rather, is 'Am I merely the mind?' (or a sum of perceptions), or even the question, 'Do I really exist?'. Until Descartes can prove the physical world is real, his mental experiences are all that are real to him. This is an important point when he later comes to distinguish between the mind and body (remember: Descartes believes in the existence of two separate substances (mind and matter) – he is a 'mind–body dualist', not a 'brain–body dualist'!). The brains-in-vats scenario, therefore, represents a modern-day sceptical equivalent of Descartes's evil demon argument which does not require us to assume the existence of immaterial substance (i.e. soul or spirit).

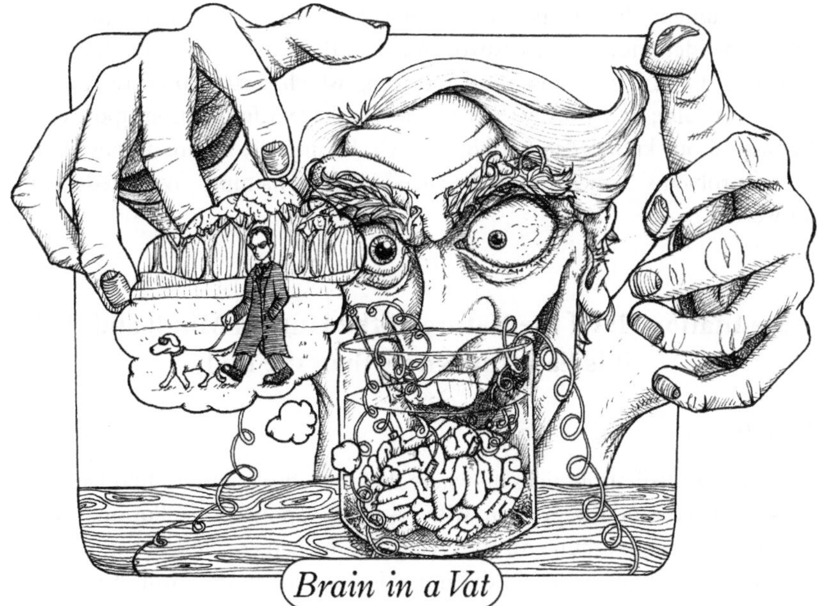
Brain in a Vat

Summary

Curiously, regarding all these questions which he has raised, Descartes is at this stage at something of a loss, for he says, 'I have certainly nothing to say in reply to such reasonings'.[12] This is an example of one of Descartes's attempts to draw the reader into the process of reasoning. Instead of saying, 'As I will later argue, the answer to these doubts can be found . . .', he attempts to create a sense of there being a shared problem, as if to say, 'Well, dear reader, where do we go from here?' The *method of doubt* thus proves quite a good tool for storytelling.[13] So, for the purposes of arriving at one thing certain, he will suppose that 'the heavens, the air, the earth, colours, shapes, sounds, and all external things that we see, are only illusions and deceptions'[14] and that he will consider himself as 'having no hands, eyes, flesh, blood or senses'.[15]

For, even if he is not able to arrive at absolutely certain knowledge, he may at least 'take great care not to accept into my belief anything false'.[16] This is the essence of his method of doubt – that is, the means whereby he hopes to achieve some form of reliable truth.

Descartes's main purpose in this first Meditation has been to undermine our commonly held beliefs regarding reality and our certainty regarding our knowledge of it. Furthermore, he has also shown that the importance of these arguments lies in their identifying the exact source of our problems. Firstly, he identifies the untrustworthiness of the senses; secondly, that we do not seem to have a means of guaranteeing which perceptions are real, and which are false; and thirdly, that we do not have a foundation upon which to base all our knowledge (without which, he implies, we are doomed). It is these problems which he will spend the remaining five Meditations answering.

Meditation II: Of the Nature of the Human Mind; and that it is Easier to Know than the Body

Introduction

The second Meditation picks up where the first left off, and we find Descartes in determined mood to press on with his quest. Applying his illusion, dreaming, and deception arguments, he recalls that he had concluded not only that it was possible that the world did not exist (at least in the form in which he took it to), but also that his body, because it was a part of the physical world, might not exist either. Therefore, the 'Descartes' that begins the second day's Meditation is dramatically less substantial than the one which began the first. Nonetheless, he is determined to continue doubting, even if it produces nothing more certain than the conclusion that 'there is nothing certain in the world.'[17]

The Evil Demon (Part Two) and the Cogito

Demons probably never really get the credit they deserve. With their reputation for evil, ill-will, and general malevolence, it is often overlooked what positive purpose their existence may occasionally serve. Certainly, without the concept of such a being, Descartes might have never arrived at his most famous utterance.

Having so far doubted the existence of the world and, more drastically, his own body, Descartes ultimately comes to question the nature of his own existence. For, he asks,

> Am I so dependent on body and senses that I cannot exist without them?[18]

It is a question which many philosophers have asked, and it continues to play an important role to this day. Am I just the mind? Is it possible that consciousness can exist without physical embodiment? Is there something such as a soul that might survive death? All these questions, as I mentioned in the Introduction, are of central importance to Descartes. As a religious believer, he is interested in proving two main points: firstly, that the mind (or soul) is the true essence of the human being;[19] secondly, that it is possible to conceive of this essence as existing separately from the body. But how does he set about doing this?

The key step lies in the role played by the evil demon. Descartes points out, quite rightly, that however powerful this evil, deceiving demon is, while he (Descartes) is being deceived, it is at least true that he (Descartes) exists.

> There is therefore no doubt that I exist, if he deceives me; and let him deceive me as much as he likes, he can never cause me to be nothing, so long as I think I am something. So that, after having thought carefully about it, and having scrupulously examined everything, one must then, in conclusion, take as assured that the proposition: *I am, I exist*, is necessarily true, every time I express it or conceive of it in my mind.[20]

This is the big breakthrough for Descartes because, whatever else is the case, it must be true that while he is thinking, he must exist. This is famously summed up in the Latin phrase – the *Meditations* was originally published in Latin, remember – *Cogito ergo sum*: 'I think, therefore I am'. Ironically, we don't actually find this phrase in the *Meditations* itself, but in another of Descartes's writings, the *Discourse on Method*.[21] However, the conclusion reached here is the same one, and the argument is most commonly referred to simply as the *Cogito* (which I shall call it from now on).

A Thinking Thing

Having decided that he must exist, Descartes then goes on to ask what in fact this means. For, it's all very well being absolutely certain that 'I exist', but what is the nature of this 'I'? First of all he rejects common definitions – such as 'man' and 'rational animal' – because they lead to yet other questions and wrangles about definition (what we mean by 'man', 'rational', and so on). So, restricting himself solely to those ideas which occurred to him when he considered his direct experience of himself, he concludes that he seems to be two things: a body, which is composed of physical parts; and a soul (or mind), which seems to possess the capacity for being conscious, having sensations, making decisions, etc.

However, having decided this, he recalls the evil demon scenario and its potential to deceive us. Now, as he has already pointed out, it is possible for him to conceive of himself as existing without a body, and that its existence may be part of a dream or some great illusion. Furthermore, many of the various activities of which he is capable – eating, walking, seeing, etc. –seem to be dependent upon the existence of the body (and therefore cannot properly be said to exist separately from it). But what, then, is his true nature?

> Another attribute is thinking, and I here discover an attribute which does belong to me; this alone cannot be detached from me. *I am, I exist*: this is certain; but for how long? For as long as I think, for it might perhaps happen, if I ceased to think, that I would at the same time cease to be or to exist. I now admit nothing which is not necessarily true: I am therefore, precisely speaking, only a thing which thinks, that is to say, a mind, understanding, or reason, terms whose significance was hitherto unknown to me.[22]

This is another vital step for Descartes. Having assured himself of the certainty of one thing – the truth of the *Cogito* argument – he has now also identified that one essential activity which defines him: thinking. He is not an eating thing, a breathing thing, a dancing thing, a practical-joke-playing thing, or a stamp-collecting thing, for none of these activities can conceivably exist without the body or the physical world (whereas, he argues, the activity of thinking can). And what is a thinking thing? It is

> a thing that doubts, perceives, affirms, denies, wills, does not will, that imagines also, and which feels.[23]

Now, of these pure activities of the soul, some are more trustworthy than others, because what they deal with is less reliant upon the idea of some 'outside' world. As you may remember, this is the reason why Descartes prefers mathematics to geography: the first deals with pure ideas alone, whereas the second relies, to some extent, on the accuracy of information which we receive through the senses. Accordingly, then, Descartes favours those mental activities which have little or nothing to do with the senses. Thus, the imagination, which relies to some extent on the reality of physical things (of which it forms images), is to be trusted no more than our perceptions of the external world itself (i.e. at this stage of his argument, not at all!).

The Piece of Wax

Having arrived at these conclusions about himself, his true nature, and which activities of the mind are trustworthy, Descartes nonetheless admits that the external world still seems more apparent and easily understood than his own mind – even though he has just seemingly proved to himself that the opposite is true. However, according to his arguments, he can only really be sure that he exists and possesses knowledge of his own nature; the existence of the external world, on the other hand, is doubtful, and its true nature difficult to comprehend. Why, then, are we tempted to think the opposite (i.e. that the world is more easily known than ourselves)? Descartes puts this down to force of habit: we are more used to thinking of the world as 'real', and less used to examining our own mental nature. But, having come to interesting and useful conclusions about the 'internal' world, he now begins to wonder what the nature of this 'external' world is.[24]

As an example, Descartes considers a piece of wax 'which has just been taken from the hive'.[25] He lists its qualities – its taste, smell, colour, texture, etc. – before placing it near a flame.

> What remained of its taste is expelled, the smell disappears, its colour changes, it loses its shape, it grows bigger, becomes liquid, warms up, one can hardly touch it, and although one taps it, it will no longer make any sound. Does the same wax remain after this change?[26]

If the wax loses all these qualities after being heated, what is there that defines its true nature? We might imagine it to be, Descartes says, a sort of substance without qualities that has a certain shape, is flexible and movable. However, when we really think about it, we do not understand the wax by being able to imagine it in one way or another, but rather by being able to comprehend its behaviour under different conditions.

> I must therefore agree that I could not even conceive by means of the imagination what the wax is, and that it is my understanding alone which conceives it.[27]

Therefore, knowledge – even of the physical world – does not come from the information which we receive through the senses, but through the role which the mind plays in understanding that information. It is this latter view which is what makes Descartes a *rationalist*, as opposed to the former one, which would make him an *empiricist*.

This is an extremely important stage in Descartes's argument. First of all, what is taking place is a switch in emphasis: from thinking that the 'external' world is more easily understood than our own 'internal', mental one, Descartes arrives at the opposite conclusion. The world of mental perceptions is most easily understood because we have direct access to it (to our perceptions and ideas); however, the external world can only be accessed *indirectly* through its interaction with the senses, and the creation of perceptions which are meant to *stand for* or represent these physical things (the ability to do which Descartes calls the 'imagination'[28]). However, as Descartes shows with the wax example, such perceptions can be misleading: the wax is solid, now it is liquid; it is yellow, now it is translucent; and so on. The *true* nature of the wax does not

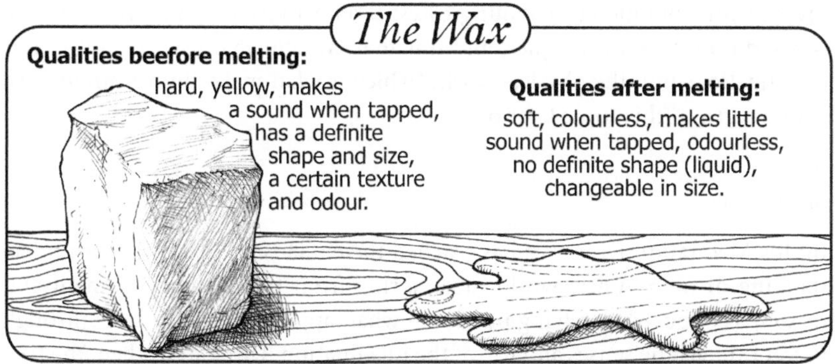

THEREFORE: We cannot understand the wax merely in terms of its possessing certain physical properties because these are changeable!

therefore consist in what we can understand of it through smell, sight, taste, etc., but rather through reason and logical deduction. Furthermore, the more our knowledge of something is arrived at through purely logical and mathematical principles, the more certain it will be. Therefore, since knowledge of the external world relies to some extent on sense perception (which can be misleading), the most certain and easily knowable things are *those whose truth does not rely on sense perception.*

The analysis of the wax has therefore allowed Descartes to reach the following conclusions:

1. The imagination (in Descartes's sense of the term) provides us with misleading impressions of the 'external' world.
2. However, certain ideas within the mind can be known with much greater certainty than perceptions which stem from 'outside' of the mind.
3. Therefore, the mental world can be known with much greater certainty than the physical one.
4. The most certain knowledge is based upon contemplation of ideas alone, and does not involve the evidence of the senses. Therefore, the more we rely upon sense perception, the more *uncertain* our knowledge will be; the more independent of sense experience our knowledge is, the more *certain* it will be.

It is tempting, here, to see Descartes as being someone who would frown upon scientific experiment (because experiment relies on sense perception). However, this is not the case. He is not arguing that we do not need experiment – on the contrary, his own interests show that he was a keen empirical investigator – but merely that our greatest certainty resides in knowledge which is based on *rational* principles, and it is these which we must seek out in our investigations into the physical world (which is what makes him a *rationalist*). I will return to this topic later on.

Summary

In this Meditation Descartes has reached the conclusion that a clearer understanding of the physical world must spring from the use of judgement and reason, as opposed to relying purely on what 'appears to be the case' through perception via the senses and use of the imagination. Ultimately, then, the true nature of things in the external world is not revealed 'through seeing them and touching them, but only because we conceive them in thought'.[29]

The other important consequence of this finding for Descartes is that, since the greatest understanding of things comes via the intellect, how much easier and certain must our knowledge of our own minds be than that of the physical world. The mind and its contents, therefore, are more easily known than the world and *its* contents. Thus, in identifying his essential nature as a 'thinking thing', and concluding that this activity – in its purest form – has nothing to do with the 'outside' world, he is able to lay the foundations for arguing that mind and body are separate and distinct substances (of which, more soon).

Meditation III: Of God; that He Exists

Introduction

The role played by God in philosophical arguments has diminished almost to nothing in modern-day philosophy (outside philosophy of religion, of course). However, in Descartes's day, religious belief was the norm and atheism almost non-existent. Two of Descartes's philosophical contemporaries, the German Wilhelm Leibniz and the Dutchman Baruch Spinoza, both incorporated the notion of a greater being into their philosophical systems, while the Irish philosopher Bishop George Berkeley assumed a world where all existing things were thoughts in the mind of God.[30] However, as religious belief has declined – and atheism and agnosticism increased – philosophy has concentrated on forms of justification which do not rely on appeal to the divine. Another reason for this, however, lies in the fact that for God to be able to act as a guarantee of anything, you must first prove that He exists.[31] It is this goal that Descartes sets himself in the third Meditation.

Clear and Distinct Ideas

In the two Meditations covered so far, Descartes has occasionally talked about how *clear* an idea is, or of *clearly and distinctly* perceiving that something is the case. However, up until now, he has not provided an analysis of what this means, or given any justification of the concepts. However, since this will be important in the discussion that is to follow (concerning the existence of God), he sets about doing so now.

Firstly, he asks, 'what is required to make me certain of something?'[32] In relation to the *Cogito*, 'there is nothing except a clear and distinct perception of what I affirm'.[33] And so,

> consequently it seems to me that I can already establish as a general rule that all the things we conceive very clearly and distinctly are true.[34]

So, taking the truth of the *Cogito* argument as a standard against which to measure all other forms of knowledge, Descartes argues that it is these qualities which it possesses – its clarity and distinctness – which guarantee its being true. Therefore, in examining the contents of his mind, Descartes finds that some ideas appear more clear and distinct than others. For instance, the ideas which he formerly held to be true about the existence of objects in the physical world now seem much less well-formed than those involving mathematics. In fact, mathematical and logical ideas seem so clear and distinct that the only thing which could convince him that they were not true would be if the evil demon argument were true – which is why, ultimately, he needs to prove that God exists and is not a deceiver (i.e. God has not created him in order that he should be easily deceived about such certainties).

However, before I move on to that topic, there remains something more to be said about clear and distinct ideas. The idea, as it is presented in the *Meditations*, is rather vague and is dealt with briefly. In fact, it seems that all it amounts to is the assertion that some ideas appear more *self-evidently true* than others. We can expand upon this definition, however, if we consider some of Descartes's comments elsewhere in his writings. For instance, in *The Principles of Philosophy*, he provides a more detailed explanation:

> I term that clear which is present and apparent to an attentive mind, in the same way as we assert that we see objects clearly when, being present to the regarding eye, they operate upon it with sufficient strength. But the distinct is that which is so precise and different from all other objects that it contains with itself nothing but what is clear.[35]

Basically, if I said to you, 'Do you see that cat over there?' and it was only two feet away from you, and it was broad daylight, and there was only one cat in the room, etc., then you could be said to 'clearly perceive' the cat. Now, if I said, 'Do you see that cloud which looks like a cat?' and the clouds were constantly shifting, and the light was fading, and it only looked like a certain one-eared, one-eyed cat that I had when I was a child, etc., then you could say that 'the resemblance of the cloud to a cat is not clearly perceptible'. So, part of the concept of the clarity of an idea involves how apparent it is, and to what extent the idea forces itself upon your attention without you having to look for it. Descartes himself uses the example of being in pain: if you have toothache, for example, there is no sense in which you can wonder, 'Am I really in pain? Is it really pain which I feel?'. The sensation is definitely present, and is in this sense 'clear'.

So much for *clear*, but what about *distinct*? This seems to concern the extent to which an idea is independent of other ideas. So, for instance, mathematical concepts are very distinct – you could not confuse '3' with '4', for instance (at least, once you have learnt these concepts). However – to use Descartes's example once more – the knowledge one has of being in pain, while it is clear, is not distinct. To illustrate this, think of having toothache. You may feel the pain intensely, but as to where the problem is, exactly, or what the cause is, the pain itself gives you a confused and imprecise idea (you may feel an infection of one of your back teeth as a more general pain spreading over the side of your face). One interesting point which arises from this is that while ideas can be clear and distinct (the best sort), or clear and not so distinct (the not-so-good sort), they cannot be *unclear* and distinct. In other words, if an idea is distinct, it must also be clear.[36] So, if you don't confuse the concepts of '3' and '4', it is partly because their meaning is clear to you, and they are distinct because you can clearly distinguish between the meanings of the two terms.[37]

The Division of Ideas

Having established the reason why particular ideas are more certain than others, Descartes now sets about grouping the contents of his mind under certain categories according to the role each has in our mental life.

The first division that he makes is a threefold one involving *images* (or *ideas* as he calls them[38]), *volitions or affections*, and *judgements. Images* are simply representations of things (such as an image of a man, or a cloud, or a blue car) and need not in themselves be false. Just having a mental image of a blue car is not in itself mistaken – unless, of course, it refers to some specific intention (such as thinking it is in the garage, which might be mistaken – not least because both garage and car might not even exist!). Secondly, *volitions* (things which involve acts of will) and *affections* (how we feel about things) are similarly immune to being false. The reason for this is that simply wanting or not wanting something (desiring a new car, for instance) is not something that can be false (for, even if it turns out that the car does not exist, at least it is still true that I desire it). The same thing goes for *affections*: not liking cheese is something which can still be the case even if it turns out that what I thought was cheese was only actually 'virtual cheese', fed to me by an evil scientist as I sit as a brain in a vat. (*Can* brains 'sit'? Well, you get the idea.). However, the third main category – that of *judgements* – does in fact rely upon the existence of things outside the mind (with one important exception, which I shall come to in a moment). For instance, if I say, 'There is a blue sofa in the next room', that is something which can be true or false (either because there is or isn't a sofa in the next room, or – more drastically – because the real world doesn't exist, and it's all a dream, or some other type of illusion). Philosophers would say, therefore, that statements that can be true or false have *truth value*.

The Division of Ideas

Type of Idea	*Definition*	*Example*	*Truth Value*	*Related to the External World?*
Images	Mental Representations of things	An image of a blue car	None (simply having an image is neither true nor false)	Not necessarily (it may not exist!)
Affections and Volitions	Expressions of desire, or like or dislike, towards something	I would like to own a blue car. That's a nice shirt. I hate cheese.	None (having a desire or attitude is neither true not false)	Not necessarily (it may not exist!)
Judgements	Propositions	There is a blue car outside my house.	Yes	Mostly . . .

As you can see, only judgements have any truth value, while the mere fact that we have an image, or a desire, need have no bearing on anything at all ('I like cheese' is not saying, 'cheese exists' – it may only be dream cheese!).

Furthermore, the images, affections, and volitions that we find in our minds do not necessarily have any connection with the external world (I may have made them all up). Judgements, however, mostly concern the existence of circumstances independent of me. So, when I say, 'the car is blue', I am also asserting, 'there exists a physical object that corresponds to my idea which exists independently of me'. However, not all judgements are of this sort (I shall return to this in a moment).

Having established that judgement concerning ideas is the only category that directly concerns knowledge, Descartes sets about subdividing this category according to how these ideas originate. The three categories of ideas are *factitious*, *adventitious*, and *innate*. *Factitious* ideas are ones that I might invent myself – the examples Descartes gives are 'sirens, hippogryphs, and all other similar chimera'[39] – by which he basically means 'any imaginary thing that I can think of that has no basis in reality' (i.e. which has been created in my mental *fact*-ory). Secondly, *adventitious* ideas come from outside the mind and have an external cause for their existence – Descartes's examples are hearing a noise, seeing the sun, or feeling heat. Lastly, there are *innate* ideas. These have no external cause and are not created by the mind, but are rather there from the start (i.e. from birth). Examples would be mathematical concepts: Descartes would argue that we do not discover them from experience. For instance, it would be odd to think of us arriving at the concept of '3' by constantly coming across groups of things and finding that, yes, indeed, *that* object and *that* object and *that* object do in fact make '3'. Numbers are not that sort of concept. On the other hand, however, we do not merely devise mathematical concepts as convenient ways of categorizing the world (as we might invent the rules of a game, or name something). There is no logical reason why game rules can't change, or why we can't rename a certain thing, but if mathematics were like that then the whole possibility that we could use it to describe reality (via physics, etc.) would completely collapse.[40]

The keener among you may have noticed that there would appear to be a contradiction here. Earlier I stated that innate ideas may *mostly* be classed under *judgements*, which in turn I defined as those ideas which can be true or false since, in general, they involve some assertion about the real world (e.g. 'there is a blue car outside my house'). However, the definition of innate ideas that I have just given implies that certain ideas can be true *independent* of outside circumstances. So, for instance, '2 + 2 = 4' will be true whether or not the two pairs of objects I am counting actually exist (or whether, for instance, I have failed to notice that there are actually five objects). We may say then, more precisely, that innate ideas represent a unique category of judgement: firstly, they are judgments (which thus have truth value); secondly, their truth is independent of external circumstances. Therefore, they may be contrasted on the one hand with things which do not in themselves have any truth value (images, affections, and volitions), and on the other hand with judgements whose truth is reliant upon circumstances in the 'external' world (i.e. judgements concerning factitious and adventitious ideas).

The Division of Judgements

Origin of Idea	*Definition*	*Example*	*Truth in relation to outside world*
Factitious	Ideas which seem to have been created within the mind[41]	A unicorn, a hippogryph[42]	Dependent
Adventitious	Ideas which would appear to have originated from outside.	Representations of the external world (e.g. an image of the sun, sensation of heat, etc.).	Dependent
Innate	Ideas which are true independently of external circumstances, not self-created or originating from outside	$2 + 2 = 4$. The internal angles of a triangle add up to 180°	Independent

The above table shows that, of these three categories of idea, only innate ideas are independent of external circumstances. Factitious ideas need to be referred to the outside world to be true (or not), and whether adventitious ideas are true depends on the degree to which our senses are reliable, etc. However, innate ideas are independent of the world in that the truths which they embody are certain, regardless of whether our senses deceive us, or whether we are living in a permanent dream.

It is worth us spending a moment or two, here, as the concept of innate ideas is an important one not only for Descartes, but for other rationalist philosophers as well (in fact, the question of whether or not innate ideas actually exist was a central point of difference between rationalist and empiricist philosophers). However, the idea was not new and may be said to have originated with Plato, who believed that certain ideas were not learnt, but merely 'remembered'. Plato believed in reincarnation and that our knowledge of innate ideas was somehow instilled in us between lives.[43] However, Descartes – being a

Christian – based his view on the idea that God somehow implanted the ideas in our mind, or that their existence was a consequence of His having created the human mind in a certain way. This is not to say that Descartes thought that we were born *already knowing* them, but merely that, through experience, it was possible to discover them (although their truth was independent of experience). In this sense, we may say that innate ideas are *a priori* (a Latin term meaning 'from what is before'), the opposite of which would be *a posteriori* (meaning 'from what comes after'), referring to knowledge which is dependent upon experience.[44]

The Origin of Things

Having finalized his categories, Descartes first asks what reason we have for considering that the ideas of external objects that we possess actually originate from objects which truly exist independently of us. The first argument he considers is that the belief that such objects exist is 'taught me by nature'.[45] But what can this amount to? In invoking nature, we are not talking about our 'natural reason' – i.e. our ability to see when something is clearly and distinctly true, or the 'natural light' as he calls it – for he has already argued that there are plausible, logical reasons for not automatically accepting the existence of such objects. What people commonly mean when they use 'nature' in this way, however, is that it seems 'natural' to believe something (as in, 'Naturally, I assumed that you had let the cat out'). However, as Descartes has already shown, it is just these sorts of 'natural' beliefs or impulses that we ought to be on our guard against (he returns to this topic in more detail in the final Meditation).

The second argument that he considers is that these images, since they do not seem to originate from my own will (I am not conscious of creating them), must originate from outside (and so are trustworthy representations of objects that actually exist). However, there are two reasons for rejecting this: firstly, just because I am not aware of producing such images does not mean that there is not in fact some power within me that is responsible (such as happens with dreaming); secondly, even if such objects *are* the cause, this does not mean that such images are true representations of them, since quite often – as the argument from illusion has shown – our senses can present misleading information on the true nature of the world (consider mirages, bent sticks, etc.).

Moving on, Descartes now examines the ideas themselves with a view to determining if there is any quality in them that might help decide whether they may exist separately from him. Firstly, he notes that some ideas seem to contain more 'reality' than others. For instance, ideas which represent actual substances seem to possess more 'objective reality' than, as he says, 'those which represent to me only modes or accidents'.[46] For instance, a chair is more objectively real than a shadow, or a patch of reflected light. The reason for this is that there is an underlying substance to the chair which seems to persist through the various changes in perception that I have in relation to it. In other words, the light may change, the colour, shape, and size (in relation to position) may alter, but there is something which seems to persist through these surface changes. As with the wax, there would seem to be some substance which possesses these changing features, and which our intellect can comprehend. Contrast this with the changing features themselves – the shadow and light – which seem less 'substantial'. Their existence seems more fleeting, relative, and changeable, and there seems to be an important sense in which they are dependent on other things for their existence. Put simply, then, the idea of the chair is more substantial – possesses more reality – because it acts as the basis for the less substantial ideas. (I will return to this distinction later when I look at 'primary and secondary qualities', as they are termed.)

Ultimately, Descartes also notes that the idea of God is more real than even the idea of physical substances.

> Moreover, the idea by which I conceive a God who is sovereign, eternal, infinite, unchangeable, all-knowing, all powerful and universal Creator of all things outside himself, that idea, I say, has certainly more objective reality in it than those by which finite substances are represented to me.[47]

You may say that this still leaves the idea of what is 'real' somewhat undefined, and partly subjective (a criticism to which we shall return later). Slowly, however, Descartes is creeping towards his main objective in this Meditation: might he be able to prove the existence of God?

The Trademark Argument

Having divided up the contents of the mind and shown that some ideas are more real than others, it remains for Descartes to prove that God is not a deceiver. This is important, you may recall, because without this proof, everything which he has so far established – the *Cogito*, that he is a thinking thing, that that which is clearly and distinctly perceived must be true – will all be for nothing, for it may yet be true that he is the subject of deception. To disprove this, therefore, he must not only prove God's existence, but must account for the fact that God so created us that we occasionally seem to fall into error. The second of these objectives he reserves for the fourth Meditation, but the first he tackles now (though it is only the first of two arguments that he presents for the existence of God).

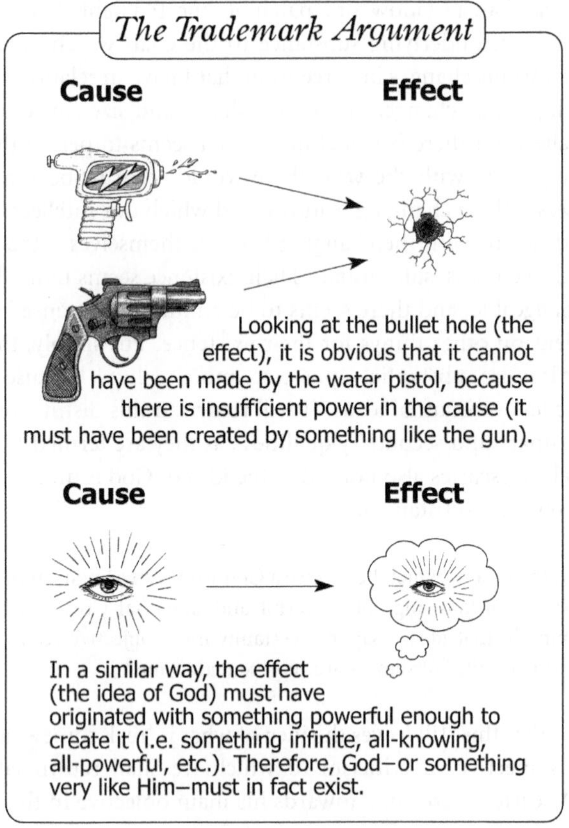

The Trademark Argument
Cause
Effect
Looking at the bullet hole (the effect), it is obvious that it cannot have been made by the water pistol, because there is insufficient power in the cause (it must have been created by something like the gun).
Cause
Effect
In a similar way, the effect (the idea of God) must have originated with something powerful enough to create it (i.e. something infinite, all-knowing, all-powerful, etc.). Therefore, God–or something very like Him–must in fact exist.

The first step of the argument lies in the notion that there is 'as much reality' in a cause as in its effect. What does he mean by this? To illustrate his point, think of a good-sized bullet hole. Now, if someone wants to know which type of gun fired the bullet, and I said, 'This one' (producing a water pistol), then you would laugh. An average water pistol is not capable of producing such a hole.[48] Another way of saying this is that 'there is inadequate potential in the proposed cause (the water pistol) to produce the effect (the bullet hole)'. So, in rejecting the water pistol as a possible cause of the bullet hole, we are employing something similar to Descartes's principle. 'Show me the real gun,' you might say, 'the one which is *actually capable* of making this hole.' Similarly, then, if we replace the bullet hole with the *idea* of God, the gun with God Himself, and the power of the gun with the idea of perfection, then we can begin to understand what Descartes is getting at. If, with any of the ideas in his mind – but especially that of God – Descartes can conclude that he was not the cause of it (and it cannot have originated from nothing), then whatever that idea implies was its creator must necessarily exist (for this reason, this is known as the *causal adequacy principle*).

Of the ideas in his mind, most of them could be said to have originated from Descartes himself, since they do not possess anything which he himself does not possess. The ideas he has of men, animals, angels, physical objects – all, it can be argued, could be formed by piecing together ideas that he has of himself, or that he might easily have created. However, the idea of God seems to be different.

> By the name God I understand an infinite substance, eternal, immutable, independent, omniscient, omnipotent, and by which I and all the other things which exist (if it be true that any such exist) have been created and produced.[49]

Such a concept, Descartes argues, cannot have originated with him because he is just a finite being, whereas the idea of God that he has represents an infinite one. This said, Descartes anticipates some objections to his argument:

1. Firstly, that he himself does not possess a true idea of infinity (and so the idea of an infinite being does not require an infinite cause). This he rejects because, he says, if he did not really possess the idea of infinity, how else could he get the idea that he himself is imperfect and finite (without a perfect and infinite being with which to compare himself)?[50]
2. Next, the idea cannot have originated out of nothing, because – unlike, for instance, the ideas of 'heat' and 'cold' – it is 'very clear and distinct'.[51] So, even if he can't comprehend such an idea – which he admits he cannot – it has to be there in some real sense in order for it to act as a real comparison.
3. Perhaps, even though he is not infinite, all-powerful, etc., he may *potentially* be so, so that the idea might originate from the idea of his own future potential. However, he rejects this also because a finite thing (such as he is) does not approach being infinite by degrees. That is, no matter how much his own power and knowledge increase, they can only ever get *bigger*, not become *limitless* (which is the true idea of infinity).

Having listed and rejected these objections, Descartes now considers another possible problem with the argument. What if there were no God? What other cause could there be for his own existence? Descartes lists three possible sources of origin: himself, his parents, or another source less perfect than God.

Firstly, then, himself: is Descartes his own creator? There are all sorts of reasons why Descartes rejects this. First of all, he argues, if he was his own creator, wouldn't he have given himself all the perfections of which he has ideas (oh, and a beautiful wife, lots of money, a mansion on the Italian Riviera, and a sports car – I'm assuming that time is not a constraint here)? Also, he points out that the creative force behind something must also constantly maintain its existence (as God is said to sustain Himself and the whole universe). However, since he is not aware of any power in himself that might accomplish that, he finally rejects this possibility.

Secondly, what about some other cause less powerful than God? This Descartes rejects because such a cause would beg the question of what created *that* cause, and so on, until we would have to suppose some all-powerful *first* cause which was at the same time capable of sustaining its own and the universe's existence from moment to moment.

Lastly, Descartes considers the possibility that his parents created him. While there is a sense in which this is literally true (his parents are responsible for his physical conception), there is no sense in which either can be said to be responsible for his continued moment-to-moment existence, or the creation of him as a thinking thing (that is, a mind or soul).

So, having rejected these other possibilities, Descartes finally arrives at the conclusion that God is not only the cause of his existence, but also the cause of his having the idea of God in the first place.

Summary

Having identified the idea of God as the idea that possesses the most 'objective reality', Descartes has spent the whole of this (quite long and difficult) Meditation in attempting to prove that he could not have got the idea from anywhere else. Having done this, and because of the principle that there must be as much reality in the cause as in its effect, the presence of the idea of an infinite being proves that such a being must, in fact, exist. Just as a workman leaves some sign of his having created something – as a painter signs a canvas – so God has left his *trademark* via the idea of Himself. In addition to this, since the concept Descartes has is of a perfect being, God cannot in fact be a deceiver (and have purposefully created Descartes as a flawed being), since 'deceit stems necessarily from some defect', and the concept he has of God includes the attribute of perfection.[52] God, therefore, not only exists, but is also a good and non-deceiving creator. How, then, does it happen that Descartes is sometimes deceived or falls into error? This is the subject of the next Meditation.

Meditation IV: Of Truth and Error

Introduction

So far Descartes has achieved a lot of what he set out to do: he has identified the weaknesses in our current state of knowledge; he has shown that if we are to achieve certainty then we must base our knowledge on something absolutely certain, and discovered that thing (the truth of the *Cogito*); he has established that when we clearly and distinctly perceive things, we cannot go wrong; and he has provided assurances that God exists and is not responsible for any errors that we may commit in our search for knowledge. However, he now needs to find the reasons why such errors *do* in fact occur.

The Reason for Error

Firstly, Descartes notes that he has not only the idea of God, but also that of God's opposite – nothing, or non-existence. Furthermore, he seems to find himself midway between these two extremes: he is not in any way as perfect as God, nor is he totally imperfect. He is a finite, limited being, and although God has created him with adequate senses and mental apparatus, they are nonetheless finite. If, then, his mind and senses are not faulty, what is the reason for error? Descartes concludes that

> my being mistaken arises from the fact that the power which God has given me of discerning the true from the false is not infinite in me.[53]

In other words, it is the scope of his understanding which is limited. However, there is still a problem. When we make mistakes, it is not simply because we are limited in our knowledge, but rather because we don't know something that we *ought* to know. So, I cannot know exactly what another person is thinking (I cannot have the same access to his thoughts as I have to my own). However, while not knowing such a thing may be a limitation, it is not a mistake (to assume that he is thinking something which he is not would be a mistake). Limitation in itself is therefore not itself responsible for error, and so the problem seems to resurface: why do we fall into error?

Next, Descartes wonders, since God 'always wills what is best',

> is it more advantageous then for me to be deceived than not to be deceived?[54]

First of all, he replies, we should not really second-guess God. We cannot know what He knows, and for all *we* know there is a good reason why our understanding is limited. Secondly, we might consider the bigger picture, for while our understanding seems imperfect to us, in relation to the whole of creation (of which we don't have an overview), it might fit God's plans perfectly. This second argument is a bit like saying, 'Birds don't have opposable thumbs, but they don't really need them for the day-to-day business of being-a-bird'.

So much for the reasons why God isn't to blame, but what about the reasons why we are prone to fall into error? The argument put forward by Descartes involves his definition of the separate roles of the understanding and the will. Our power to understand is limited, but – as he has already argued – there may be good reasons for that. Anyway, for a finite thing, it is sufficient for its purposes (and, as we have seen, limitation is not the same thing as error). However, regarding our power of will, he can see no reason why we should not consider it perfect and unlimited. In other words, we are restricted in our understanding, memory, imagination, etc., but whatever the case, we can always say 'yes' or 'no', *do* or *not do* a thing – is there anything else in the exercise of will than this? Therefore, neither will nor understanding seems to be directly responsible for my falling into error. But if neither power is faulty, then how do they lead to mistakes? Descartes's answer is that it is due to the use that we make of them:

> Whence, then, arise my errors? From this fact alone, that the will being much more ample and extended than the understanding, I do not contain it within the same limits, but extend it also to things I do not understand, and the will being of itself indifferent to such things, very easily goes astray and chooses the bad instead of good, or the false instead of the true, which results in my falling into error or sinning.[55]

The Importance of Being Indifferent

Descartes has argued that if we can restrain our will from affirming or denying things of which we do not possess a sufficient understanding, then we can avoid falling into error. But how do we know when to withhold our judgement? The answer lies, he says, in the extent to which we feel indifferent or compelled to pass judgement. In other words, when an argument seems so logically conclusive that we feel that we must hold it to be true – as with the *Cogito* – then that is exactly the sort of feeling we should use as a guide to truth. On the other hand, if we simply feel indifferent whether something is true or not, and do not feel compelled one way or the other, then we should simply withhold our judgement.

It is important to note that the feeling of compulsion which Descartes is talking about here is not any emotional feeling or strong desire, but rather the realization that an idea is 'clearly and distinctly' true. On the other hand, the indifference he describes also has nothing to do with personal tastes or interests – I may feel 'indifferent' to finding the answer to certain questions in chemistry or physics (because I am not interested), but that does not mean that the questions involved aren't capable of being answered conclusively.

Summary

Having defended God against the charge of faulty workmanship, Descartes has managed to lay another stone of the foundations of his building of secure knowledge. Thus, if we can follow the principles that he has set out, we need not have cause to blame our limited intellect, or the fact that our will can sometimes be used to assert things beyond our understanding. Rather, if we restrict ourselves to asserting only those things of which we possess a clear and distinct understanding, then not only will we not fall into error, but we will be using both will and understanding as God intended.

Meditation V: Of the Essence of Material Things; and, Once More of God, that He Exists

Introduction

We have come a long way from the doubts of the first Meditation, and if the whole of the *Meditations* can be viewed as a sort of 'there and back again' journey, then it is at this point that we begin to sight home. In the first Meditation, Descartes's first doubts were directed at our knowledge of the real world. Now, having established a certain basis for knowledge, and set out principles whereby we may avoid going wrong, he is ready to begin tackling the subject of the true nature of the world whose existence he first called into question. However, in addition to the trademark argument he proposed in the last Meditation, Descartes presents us here with another argument for the existence of God intended to show how we are compelled to 'clearly and distinctly perceive' that He exists.

Ideas of Material Things

Up to now, Descartes has postponed answering the question of the extent to which – if at all – the physical world as we perceive it is real. However, having arrived at the point where he must now do this, his first step is not to look outside himself, but rather to examine the contents of his own mind. In doing so, he finds a number of ideas relating to objects – such as size, shape, position, motion – and these allow him to distinctly perceive how such objects might interact, move, change over time, etc. But has he produced these ideas himself, or have they originated outside him?

Firstly, he rejects the idea that he has somehow manufactured these ideas himself, because, after investigation, these objects possess properties which he had not foreseen, could not have predicted, and so could not have invented. For example, consider a triangle. If I discover some property of triangles – such as that their internal angles add up to 180° (a fact which, for argument's sake, I will suppose I do not know) – then I cannot be said to have invented that shape.

Secondly, he also dismisses the idea that I have somehow learnt these ideas through the senses (as the empiricists argue), because, if he had done so, how could he then conceive of geometrical shapes which he has never seen in material form (such as the *chiliagon*, or 'thousand-sided shape', which he will consider in the next Meditation)?

Both these objections point to the fact that the very idea of physical objects embodies mathematical principles which are independent of experience, and therefore innate. So, whether or not physical objects actually exist, the idea of them – as things with dimension, shape, duration, and motion – is a clear and distinct one. Therefore, such objects *may* exist, because we can conceive of them clearly and distinctly in this way. The essence of material things is therefore the *idea* that our understanding of them allows us (as it was with the wax). Furthermore, since this understanding is based on mathematical principles (e.g. size, weight, change over time, etc.), the ideas contained therein cannot be false. Of course, we may make mistakes involving maths and geometry (when adding up or multiplying, calculating shape, etc.), or we may even make mistakes as to how such ideas relate to the real world (e.g. we may imagine something to be structured differently than it really is – think of the ongoing investigations into the nature of the atom in physics). However, the principles involved remain the same, and as long as we base our knowledge on clear and distinct perceptions, then those perceptions will be – within limits – relatively trustworthy.

The Ontological Argument

Suddenly, it occurs to Descartes how he might adapt all this talk of triangles to supply another argument for the existence of God. The way he does this is through distinguishing between the concepts of *existence* and *essence*. In regard to physical objects, we have seen that we can have the idea of objects without necessarily supposing that they actually exist. For instance, I can think of a golden pyramid, and that object must possess all the properties that pyramids possess (those properties are *essential* to it – it would not be a pyramid without them). However, whether such a pyramid *actually* exists, we do not know. So, we may distinguish between the *idea* of a thing (its *essence*), and that thing's *existence.*

However, when we consider the idea of God, the case is somewhat different. As a triangle or a pyramid has essential properties (without which it would not be a triangle or a pyramid), so does God. Now, apart from such qualities as omnibenevolence (being all-good), omniscience (being all-knowing), and omnipotence (being all-powerful), God also possesses the property of eternal existence. However, if He didn't exist, then the idea of God would not possess this property. Therefore, since it is an essential property of the idea of God that He exists eternally, then God must exist (i.e. 'existence' must also be an essential property of God). In this way, God is different from other things we might imagine (such as golden pyramids) whose *existence* is separate from their *essence.* This is called the *ontological argument* because it involves an analysis of the concept of God's *being* or *existence* (*ontology* means literally, 'relating to the nature of being and existence').[56]

Descartes anticipates three main objections to this argument. Firstly, some might argue that we may conceive of God as not existing, and that His existence may therefore be separate from His essence. However, this cannot be so, Descartes replies, for another property of God is that of perfection, and non-existence would represent a flaw in the idea of God. Hence, since He is perfect, He must also exist.

Secondly, it may be argued that while it may not be possible to conceive of God without thinking of the idea of His existing, it does not follow that there is any such being. For instance, just because we may not conceive of mountains existing without valleys, this does not necessarily mean that any mountains or valleys actually exist. Descartes's reply to this is that, once again, the idea of God is different in that we cannot separate the idea of His existence from His other properties. Furthermore, because we can clearly and distinctly perceive that existence is necessarily part of the concept of God, then the idea must be true (i.e. it must correspond to reality).

Lastly, it may be objected that, even if the idea of God necessarily implies that He exists, it is not necessary that we think of the idea of God in the first place (so, if the idea does not exist, then neither might God). Descartes replies that whenever we think of a being greater than ourselves, then we are necessarily led to the idea of God, and contained therein is the idea of His necessarily existing. Similarly, imagine that we did not possess the idea of a triangle. Even so, it would nonetheless be true that when we consider the mathematical properties of certain shapes, we would be forced to arrive at the same idea. So, for Descartes, such ideas as 'God' and 'triangle' are similar in that they are true whether anyone is aware of them or not, because once we think of certain things, we are forced to arrive at those ideas.

The role played by God in Descartes's arguments cannot be underestimated, for, as Descartes says himself, regarding God's existence:

> certainty concerning all the other truths depends on it so absolutely that, without this knowledge, it is impossible ever to know anything perfectly.[57]

The reason for this is, once again, the possibility of an evil demon. Because, no matter how 'clear and distinct' ideas appeared to Descartes, if he did not possess the knowledge that God exists then it would still be possible that he could be mistaken in his certainty. However, with God, he is assured of the reliability of the principle of clear and distinct ideas, and can use them as a basis upon which to build his knowledge of the world and of himself.

Summary

In this Meditation, Descartes has accomplished two things. Firstly, he has shown that the essence of material objects lies in their correspondence to the principles of mathematics and geometry. All knowledge that we may possess of the physical world, therefore, must be based on these principles. Secondly, he has provided another argument for the existence of God (the ontological argument). In doing so, he has reinforced the whole structure of his arguments, and provided the last-but-one step in his search for certainty.

Meditation VI: Of the Existence of Material Things, and of the Real Distinction between the Soul and the Body of Man

Introduction

As Descartes concluded in the previous Meditation, we know that material things may exist because it is possible to clearly and distinctly conceive of them. However, proving that something *may* exist is different from proving that it *does*. For instance, we may conclude that such a thing as the Loch Ness Monster *may* exist (for it to be some sort of surviving *plesiosaur*, for example), but that does not mean that it actually *does*. So, in this Meditation, Descartes's main task is to find a conclusive argument for the existence of material things. In doing this, he also seeks to achieve something else: a clear distinction between mind and body. This view, known as *Cartesian dualism*,[58] has been implicit in much of the *Meditations* so far, but it is only at this point that Descartes explicitly states it and explores its consequences.

Note: This Meditation is quite long and difficult to summarize. The topics that Descartes raises are not completely 'clear and distinct' from one another and in talking about one thing he frequently introduces another thing from a separate topic. So, in grouping the subjects under headings I have had to change slightly, for the sake of convenience, the order in which things appear in the text, and split up topics that Descartes treats together. However, the summary is otherwise an accurate account of the text and of Descartes's arguments.

Imagination and Understanding

As we have already seen, Descartes has come to consider some faculties essential to his true nature (as a thinking thing), while others are inessential (he can do without them and still be 'Descartes'). However, as he turns his attention once more outwards in search of some guarantee that physical objects actually exist, he finds that while his power of understanding seems to be able to deal in pure concepts (such as those of maths), his imagination seems to deal only in images or representations of things. But representations of what? It is tempting to say, 'representations of material objects', but how does he know this? (It should just be noted here that by *imagination* Descartes has in mind the production of *all* mental images, and not just the use of that faculty to produce, well, *imaginary* things, such as hippogryphs.)

While he cannot at this point be certain, it nevertheless seems likely that, just as the understanding turns inwards to look upon the contents of the mind, so the imagination turns outwards to the perception of material objects. In other words, both activities need an object, and since the object of understanding is oneself (or the ideas within the mind), the object of imagination must be *something else*. He backs this argument up by pointing out that understanding and imagination are different types of activity. For instance, take the idea of a triangle: we may understand it conceptually via the understanding (e.g. through analysis of its mathematical properties), or we may rely upon a mental image. Now, this works fine for certain simple images, but what about complex ones? What about a *chiliagon* (a thousand-sided shape), Descartes asks. We would be unable to form a clear mental picture of such a shape so that, for instance, we could picture it differently from a *myriagon* (a ten-thousand-sided shape). However, through the faculty of the understanding we may conceive of the difference clearly.

The point of this argument is to show that the imagination is inessential to the pure self, and that its real use lies in dealing with images. However, since these images are not needed for any understanding of our essential self (of 'what I am'), they may be required for some sort of understanding of material things. In this sense, the imagination may act as a sort of 'go-between' for the mental and physical worlds. However, for the purposes of proving that material things exist, Descartes is unhappy with this argument as it is only really a probable one. What he is actually looking for is an utterly convincing reason why the physical world must exist.

Summary of Doubts

Descartes recalls that he once believed – before this whole business began – that sense impressions give him information regarding material objects through taste, sound, colour, etc. Might this sort of information provide him with the sort of proof that he is looking for? To find out, he says, he needs to learn more about the nature of the senses that provide him with such information.

What then follows is basically a summary of the *Meditations* to date, with an emphasis on how this all relates to the senses. Descartes's steps are as follows:

1. In line with the former things I believed, the various sense impressions that I received (heat from the sun, sensations of touch, etc.) suggested that material things actually existed.
2. Furthermore, since I could not call these objects before me or banish them at will (as I might do with imaginary things), and since the impressions that I received from them were fresher and more real than I could create myself, then this seemed to suggest that the objects indeed existed independently of me.
3. For these reasons, it seemed likely that these ideas were true representations of those objects.
4. Also, since sense impressions seemed more real than mere ideas, it appeared that all ideas must have as their stimulus something outside me.
5. As one of the objects in the world, my body seemed to be different from others in that I actually experienced the things that happened to it (pain, pleasure, etc.), whereas for other objects this did not happen.

6. This suggested that I was related to my body in a way that I was not related to other objects, and that I could not be separated from it.
7. Due to this connection, therefore, just as my body teaches me that I am hungry by a certain sensation, perhaps other objects teach me as to their nature by the sensations they produce in me (e.g. that fire is hot)?
8. However, further thought showed me that this was not always the case:
   a. There were occasions when what it seemed 'natural' to assume about something was in fact false (e.g. mirages, viewing things at a distance). However, this was true not only of judgements involving 'external' things, but also of assumptions involving internal sensations (e.g. when someone feels sensation in a 'phantom limb'[59]).
   b. It seemed possible that I was dreaming, or that the same process was somehow at work even when I was 'awake'.
   c. Since I did not know who created me, there could yet have been some evil demon whose sole purpose it was to deceive me.
   d. Perhaps there was an as yet unknown faculty which falsely produced in me these perceptions of physical objects.

This summary takes us roughly up to the end of the first Meditation, at which point Descartes had more or less rejected the evidence of the senses as being untrustworthy. However, having now answered those doubts concerning his existence, the existence and nature of God, and how he may be certain of his own knowledge, he is in a better position to evaluate the evidence of the senses:

> But now that I am beginning to know myself better and to discover more clearly the author of my being, I do not think in truth that I ought rashly to accept all the things which the senses seem to teach us, but also I do not think that I ought to doubt them all in general.[60]

So, while he still doesn't trust them blindly (as he once did), he does not now wholly *distrust* them either.

Mind and Body

Now that Descartes is prepared to admit some of the evidence of the senses, he sets about defining the true relationship between the mind and the body:

> because, on the one hand, I have a clear and distinct idea of myself in so far as I am only a thinking and unextended thing, and because, on the other hand

> I have a distinct idea of the body in so far as it is only an extended thing but which does not think, it is certain that I, that is to say my mind, by which I am what I am, is entirely and truly distinct from my body, and may exist without it.[61]

In other words, body and mind are not only separate, but also represent *different types of thing*. Descartes and his contemporaries might talk about this in terms of *substance* (a technical term in philosophy meaning, roughly, 'that which possesses properties'). So, for Descartes, physical substance was not capable of thought, but possessed *extension* (this just means that it was 'extended' in different directions in space, having length, breadth, and height). The essential activity of mental substance, however, was thinking, but it was not extended in any way (in other words, it did not occupy space, possessing no size or shape). Thus, another reason why we should consider both substances as separate and distinct is that, while matter is divisible (we may cut it up into parts), mind is not (there are no 'parts' to my mind, only different activities).[62]

An important consequence of these arguments is that they can be used to reinforce the doctrine of the soul. If mind and body were inseparable, for instance, then the soul might die with the body. However, separability allows for its continued existence. Furthermore, dualism also mirrors Descartes's other assertions concerning knowledge: if dualism is true, then certainty resides with that which we truly are (i.e. our mental self), and the innate ideas and principles with which it is furnished; on the other hand, however, the physical self – which is really only a vehicle for our true self – is more closely allied with perceptual illusion and the possibility of error.

This said, at other points Descartes also seems to entertain the idea that mind and body act very closely together indeed. Our natural feelings on the matter are that I am not only in my body, as he puts it, 'like a pilot in his ship'[63] (we might also say, 'like a driver in a car'), but closer, 'indeed, so compounded and intermingled with my body, that I form, as it were, a single whole with it'.[64] If this were not the case, he argues, we would be aware of bodily sensations (such as pain and hunger) indirectly via – for example – visual knowledge (in the same way that we might notice that our car's door had been scratched), and not directly through sensation. This idea is often called the *intermingling thesis*, in that it imagines that the two substances can seep into each other (like different coloured paints), or intermix with one another (like handfuls of different coloured pebbles, perhaps). This might be said to provide a problem for Descartes (which we shall examine later) in that it is difficult to see how two so different *types* of substance *can* intermingle.

The Existence of the Physical World

While body and mind are distinct, there remain questions over the status of some of the other faculties which the mind possesses. Firstly, the faculties of perception and imagination seem in part to be intellectual (they involve a degree of intellectual activity), and yet they may also be considered in part distinct from my true self in that they are activities that my mind does in relation to physical things. The power of moving and changing bodily posture, however, seems to be merely a physical thing with no intellectual activity, and therefore would seem to belong properly to some physical substance.

Yet other faculties exist whose purpose it is passively to receive sense impressions, and others actively to produce them. Once more, however, these have no intellectual content, and would therefore seem to imply the actions of some external thing upon the mind. Now, it could be that God has placed these images in Descartes's mind, but since this would represent a sort of deception on God's part (because such images *seem* to come from external physical objects) – and, remember, God is no deceiver – then such impressions must come from the fact that Descartes in fact does possess a physical body, which is one of a number of similar physical objects which exist in a material universe.

Thus, after a long and arduous journey, Descartes finally decides

> that corporeal objects exist. However, they are perhaps not exactly as we perceive them through the senses, for perception by the senses is very obscure and confused in many ways; but at least I must admit that all that I conceive clearly and distinctly, that is to say, generally speaking, all that is comprised in the object of speculative geometry, is truly to be found in corporeal things.[65]

By 'speculative geometry', Descartes merely means the sort of abstract consideration of triangles, squares, etc., that persuaded him that the physical world was *possible*. So, like any good rationalist, Descartes is still looking at the real world somewhat suspiciously, and only really trusts the mathematical and geometric principles that govern the world, and not the world itself.

What we have here is a distinction which has become very important in the history of philosophy. Not only for Descartes, but for other rationalists – and even some empiricists[66] – knowledge of physical objects could be divided into those things which we could objectively know (size, shape, weight, etc.), and those things which were to some degree subjective (colour, texture, smell, taste, etc.). Thus, objective knowledge is *primary* and represents clear and distinct knowledge; *secondary* qualities, however, are much more closely allied to the senses, and are thus correspondingly more uncertain and changeable.

Taking a normal apple, some of its qualities are objectively measurable (the primary ones), whilst others are merely subjective (the secondary ones).

It should be noted here that this distinction is not one that Descartes employs explicitly, but is rather one that is suggested by his account of physical substance. However, later philosophers – such as Locke – formalized this distinction, and it became a point of some controversy (e.g. which qualities were primary and which secondary, what such a distinction means for our knowledge of the world, etc.). However, the distinction is beset with problems, and we shall look at these in more detail in a later section.

Natural Teachings

At this stage of the Meditation, Descartes addresses the tricky topic of what he terms 'natural teachings'. In most cases of being mistaken, Descartes is confident that, 'I have within me the means of knowing these things with certainty'.[67] For, because God is not a deceiver, Descartes has the capacity to correct his own mistakes – as long as he is careful to limit his judgements in line with his understanding. However, there are a great many cases where it would appear that we are taught certain truths by nature. But what does Descartes mean, here, by 'natural teachings'? Firstly, he does not mean what is commonly termed the 'natural light' (the 'light of reason' or power of rational thought), by which ideas are seen as clearly and distinctly true (or not). Nor, by 'nature', does he mean those things which it just so happens are true of the world (such as 'the nature of gravity'). What he does mean is those impulses by means of which the physical world (especially our own body) communicates to us. How does it do this? Well, when I am hungry, I feel a certain sensation in my stomach and I know that I need to seek out food. Similarly, when I feel pain, I know that I have to avoid the thing causing it, or to seek out that cause in order to eradicate it. On the other hand, feeling pleasure might make me seek out a certain thing in order to have that experience again. So, in this sense, nature teaches that there are objects in the world, some hurtful and some harmful, which surround our own body, and that certain actions in respect of them are good, and other actions bad. Furthermore, the perceptions that we receive from them give us a more or less correct idea of each object's nature. So, fire is hot and can cause us pain, certain foods taste nice and are good for us, and so on. Therefore, what Descartes means by 'nature' is, in a way, a type of instinctual reaction to things. In this sense, such reactions involve non-rational assumptions about the nature of the world, and furthermore, since there are a great many of them, it would be very useful to Descartes in his search for certainty for him to find some way of trusting them (at least in part).

However, in order to do this, he must find the reason why there are obvious cases where it might be argued that this instinct goes wrong. An example that Descartes gives is where we eat food that has (unknown to us) been poisoned. In one sense, the initial pleasure we feel from eating such food is misleading (the food will eventually harm us). However, we can excuse this mistake, he argues, because our natural desire (i.e. the desire to eat good-tasting and normally nutritious food) is not what harms us, but merely our ignorance of the presence of the poison.

On the other hand, there is another example which would seem to point to a deeper problem. Imagine, Descartes says, that someone who is ill has a desire to drink because they are thirsty, yet – because of their illness – to do so would in fact be harmful (such as can be the case with *dropsy*,[68] a disease whereby the body retains excess fluid in its tissues). Now, the case here is somewhat more problematic than the case of the poisoned food, because the body would seem to desire naturally what in this situation would be bad for it. Descartes says that it is tempting to compare this situation to having a faulty clock: the body, like the clock, has been designed to work in a particular way (to desire water when it is thirsty); however, owing to its faulty working (being ill), it no longer does the job it should (i.e. it resembles a broken clock).

However, Descartes rejects this analogy, because a broken or poorly designed clock would imply a bad designer (i.e. God). Furthermore, he points out that the temptation to say that ill people are like broken clocks is due to a human perception of what 'good' or 'bad' function is. In other words, we look at the fact that the body desires water even when it would be harmful to it as a malfunction of the body, when in fact the body is just functioning as it should (just because a person is *dropsical* does not mean that they cannot be thirsty). For, he says, there are times when natural teachings (such as being thirsty or hungry) would be harmful to our overall well-being and should therefore be resisted. However, just because this *can* happen, it does not mean that such impulses are wholly false.

Descartes supports this assertion by pointing out that having competing or ultimately harmful natural impulses is not in itself the problem. The mind does not receive impressions from all over the body, but only through the *common sense* (or brain).[69] So, for instance, when the nerves in the foot are stimulated somewhere along the pathway to the brain (and not in the foot itself), the sensation will be felt as if it were in the foot (even though the foot itself has not been touched). However, if the body was so set up that the mind was habitually presented with the sensation as if it were somewhere along the nerve channel, or in the brain itself, then far more harm would generally result (because most of the time the sensation would actually be in the foot). Thus, the mind only receives that sensation which – generally speaking and in most cases – is best fitted to keep it in the best of health. Similarly, in the case of dropsy,

> although dryness of the throat does not always arise, as it usually does, from drink being necessary for the health of the body, but sometimes from quite the opposite reason, as is experienced by those with dropsy, yet it is much better that it should deceive in this case, than that, on the contrary, it should always deceive when the body is well, and the same holds true in other cases.[70]

In other words, the clock is not badly designed, but – like many other aspects of the human being – merely limited in its use. It does its job, but sometimes this basic function is the wrong thing in a particular context (such as when ill with dropsy).

The point with natural teachings, therefore, is that while they are in general trustworthy, they are in the final analysis only an indication of bodily needs, sensations, etc. So, we must use our reason to arrive at decisions which are best for us, only using our natural impulses as a guide. *All* our senses can, of course, help in doing this, and something which comes from one particular source can be checked by all the others (just as hallucinations cannot be touched, and so become apparent). The fact that all the different impressions can be checked against one another via reason is therefore a further argument that God has indeed given us the wherewithal to overcome such limitations.

Out of this springs, ultimately, an answer to the dreaming argument. Our memory cannot connect the events of dreams together in the same way as it can with real life, and things in dreams tend not to behave in a way that is coherent with all that we know of the world (things just disappear without reason, people and locations change suddenly, etc.). The dreaming argument fails, therefore, when it is brought before the jury of *all* our senses and faculties.

Summary

Descartes has put a lot into this Meditation – and he has had to. Partly, the length and complexity of it stems from the fact that he is – as I've already pointed out – tying up a lot of loose ends. It is as if, as he is writing, more things that need to be said are occurring to him. Of course, as I warned at the beginning of this summary, this makes the whole Meditation somewhat difficult to follow – and especially to summarize. However, having finally reached his destination, Descartes has fulfilled all of his promises: he has found his absolute certainty, proved that there is a God (who in turn guarantees that we are not completely deceived), established a way in which we may be certain of particular things, and shown the road to gaining a true understanding of the physical world. He has also, along the way, defined the relationship between the mind and the body, and, consequently, supported the notion of the existence and immortality of the soul.

So, the journey over, he has arrived back where he began. Some things are the same – the real world still exists – but others are different. The evidence of the senses must now be taken with a 'pinch of salt', and we can only say that we really know something when we clearly and distinctly perceive it. However, our minds are more than up to the task, and our natural impulses – though limited under certain circumstances – mostly provide us with a good starting point for our enquiries.

Therefore, his work over, on the seventh day Descartes rested.

Chapter 3

Critical Themes

Introduction

How convincing have Descartes's arguments been? In my summary, I have generally spoken in a way that may suggest that they have been successful – I talk of him 'proving' this and 'establishing' that. However, I have really only done this in order to aid the explanation process, for if I had stopped to criticize those same arguments while at the same time trying to explain them, I think it would have only served to muddy the explanation. Furthermore, I sincerely think it helps, when studying philosophical arguments, to treat them with as much sympathy as possible (initially, at least). It can be very tempting, especially when considering theories of which there already exists a great deal of criticism (which is certainly true of Descartes), simply to dismiss their significance by reference to common objections. However, I don't think this really does anyone any good – least of all the student, whose main purpose in studying these theories is to deepen their own understanding and sharpen their critical skills (things which are best done at first hand by encouraging reflection).

For this reason, I have kept the summary of the *Meditations* separate from the account of critical responses to it. The former should ideally serve as an uncontroversial clarification and aide-memoire concerning the content of Descartes's main theories. However, regarding the latter, I have therefore tried to present a range of responses to the main issues raised in the *Meditations* – some of which are my own, while some come from philosophers over the last three and a half centuries or so. Once again, not everyone agrees on what is wrong with Descartes's theories, and I have tried to show that the main interest lies in treating the problems he raised as living philosophical issues (rather than simply learning *why* Descartes was 'wrong'). I have therefore entitled this chapter 'Critical Themes', because I feel that what we gain most from studying Descartes is an appreciation of the type of problems he was trying to answer, and the *real* difficulties involved in doing so. Therefore, as I suggested in the introduction at the very beginning of this book, we should see Descartes as either originating or contributing to these philosophical themes, and our own task as one of tracing their development and understanding their significance to the present day.

Objections and Replies

Just before publishing the *Meditations*, Descartes gave a copy of the manuscript to a friend and correspondent, Friar Marin Mersenne (1588–1648), requesting him to circulate it amongst scholars and theologians in order to obtain critical feedback.[1] The sets of objections raised by these various commentators, and Descartes's replies to them, were then collected in an appendix at the end of the *Meditations* (there were six sets of objections in the first edition, and a seventh set was added in the second Latin edition). This correspondence therefore not only provides us with an insight into the reactions of Descartes's contemporaries, but more importantly – for a student of Descartes – allows Descartes to expand and clarify the explanations of his key ideas. In this sense, then, we may think of them as Descartes's own footnotes to the *Meditations* (as an aid to the student, places in the text where such material is discussed appear in boxes).

Since each of the commentators often had something to say about the same topic, I have therefore grouped key objections together thematically, and discuss them as these topics arise (though an account of the key objections discussed – and some not discussed – and their relation to each Meditation, can be found in Appendix B). So, for instance, in a discussion of the *Cogito*, the discussion is based upon material taken from the second, fifth, and sixth set of objections and replies. This organization makes most sense from the general student's point of view, I think, but it should nonetheless be borne in mind that the objections come from different correspondents and do not therefore represent a coherent response to the *Meditations* as a whole (though, of course, *one set* of objections might, as it mostly represents the reaction of one person to the book – so, for instance, the third set of objections represents the criticisms of the English philosopher Thomas Hobbes (1588–1679)). These are the correspondents (more on each of them can be found in the glossary under their surnames):

List of Contributors to *Objections and Replies*

Set of Objections	*Correspondent*
1	Johannes Caterus
2	Father Marin Mersenne
3	Thomas Hobbes
4	Antoine Arnauld
5	Pierre Gassendi
6	Father Marin Mersenne
7	Pierre Bourdin

Finally, the objections and replies considered represent no more than a selection of the correspondence (which, in its unabridged form, is quite considerable – far longer than the *Meditations* itself, in fact). Thus, I think it may only be of interest to the more advanced student to seek out the complete material.

Certainty and Doubt

Scepticism and the Method of Doubt[2]

The keynote of the *Meditations* is doubt. Descartes himself sets out to doubt as much of his knowledge as he possibly can as a means of arriving at something indubitable, something absolutely certain. One of the main reasons why he attempts this is as a response to scepticism, concerning both the truths of religion *and* the possibility of knowledge generally. In doing this, Descartes would have been well-read enough to realize that many of the problems with which he was concerned stretch back to the very beginnings of philosophy itself. Therefore, in appreciating his proposed solutions, we must acquaint ourselves with their origins.

Scepticism (from the Greek, *skeptesthai*, 'to examine') is – generally and loosely speaking – the philosophical view that it is impossible to know anything with absolute certainty, or to know the world as it 'really' is. This may be contrasted with the non-philosophical sense, however, where the word indicates a general reluctance to accept anything on face value or without sufficient proof (as in 'He heard that Jim had run the 100m in under ten seconds, but he remained sceptical').

Philosophical Scepticism (we might say, with a capital 'S') began in the fifth century BC in Greece, where it became associated with certain philosophers who expressed doubts about whether we could be certain about our knowledge. Protagoras of Abdera (c. 490–c. 420 BC), for instance, is reported to have said that, 'Man is the measure of all things' (implying, possibly, that we make the world in our own image) and that, 'Concerning the Gods, I am unable to know either that they exist or that they do not exist or what form they have.'[3] Gorgias (late-fifth century BC), proposed, famously, '(1) that nothing exists; (2) that if anything exists, it cannot be known; and (3) if anything can be known, it cannot be communicated'.[4] Similar opinions were associated with those known as *sophists*, men who would hire out their skills in debate and argument to anyone for the right fee. While initially, it seems, the word was used simply to describe a form of freelance tutor, it eventually became a term of contempt, and can be found in Plato's writings – for example – as a contrast to the genuine seeker of knowledge for its own sake (the philosopher). Therefore, unlike the philosopher, the sophist believed that for the person possessing enough skill, any argument could be made to sound convincing, and that 'the truth' is simply a matter of what arguments work best to win your case.[5]

Later came *Pyrrhonism*, so called after its founder, Pyrrho of Elis, who argued that since we can never know true reality we should refrain from making judgements. His pupil, Timon of Phlius, followed this by adding that equally good reasons could be found as support for either side of any argument (so it was impossible to decide which side was right). Aenesidemus (first century BC), famously put forward ten arguments in support of the sceptical position,[6] and the *New Academy* of the second century BC, founded by Carneades (214–129 BC), taught only that some arguments were more probable than others.[7] From the first few centuries AD onwards, however, the spread of Christianity saw a diminishing in sceptical thought – mainly because, perhaps, faith and doubt do not sit well alongside one another, and believers tend to be intolerant of unbelievers – and the ancient sceptical traditions were only really rediscovered in the sixteenth century at the beginning of the Renaissance.

On the one hand, then, Descartes is seeking to combat sceptical attitudes which have existed for over two thousand years. On the other, however, he is *using* sceptical arguments positively in order to expose false beliefs and reveal things which are immune to sceptical argument. In this latter sense, we might argue that Descartes is using scepticism as a tool with which to expose the flaws in the received opinion of his day without actually attacking it directly. So, while he may appear to be seeking to identify areas of uncertainty in his current knowledge (in order to find a more secure basis for our certainty), he is also managing to undermine attitudes and opinions which are simply based on doctrine and tradition. However, the authorities would have found little to criticize in the content of the *Meditations*, and the main attack upon scholasticism which the work represents is an indirect one. In other words, in asking the reader to seek truth through their own ability to reason (rather than trusting to the teachings of the Church and the Bible), Descartes is advocating the *method* of the new science, as opposed to supporting any of its specific findings (as Galileo had, and which had got him into trouble).[8]

This positive use of scepticism is famously known as Descartes's 'method of doubt'. However, it was not a method that appealed to all the commentators, some of whom wondered whether it was advisable, or even possible to call *all* things into question (e.g. the Jesuit, Pierre Bourdin).[9] Descartes's response to this was, firstly, to argue that the state of knowledge with which he began the *Meditations* could be compared with a barrel of apples some of which were rotten. Now, he argues, in order to know *which* apples are bad, we must of course tip out the whole barrel (i.e. examine every idea), only replacing in the barrel those ideas which are sound (i.e. trustworthy or certain). However, if we do not do this, we risk the possibility that the bad apples will 'infect' the good ones, and the rot will spread (i.e. the false and uncertain ideas will cause us to make bad judgements). Rejecting everything is therefore only a preliminary caution, until those 'good or bad apples' are found. However, this analogy is not exact, for according to Descartes's method, some ideas are more trustworthy than others (thus, the *Cogito* acts as a foundation for other ideas). A better analogy might therefore be that of building a house, where we must find firm ground to lay sound foundations (the *Cogito*), and work upwards using solid bricks (clear and distinct ideas).

Secondly, Descartes points out that he is not here to provide ammunition for scepticism (which was Bourdin's main worry), but merely considering those arguments in their strongest form in order to refute them, and thus obtain the strongest certainty. This method, he argues, is similar to the methods of doctors, who 'describe the illness in regard to which they wish to teach the cure'.[10] In other words, merely to consider the reason for illness and disease (scepticism) is not to teach 'the method of falling ill' (of becoming a sceptic).[11]

In the first Meditation, Descartes presents three main sceptical arguments: the argument from illusion, the argument from dreaming, and the argument from deception. Each of these represents a progressive stage in his method of doubt, and they are therefore commonly known as the 'waves of doubt' (each going slightly further than the last). Each argument presents a slightly different problem for him, so I shall now deal with them individually.

Illusion

Firstly, the argument from illusion is one of the oldest sceptical arguments. Plato, who as we know was also a rationalist, was as equally distrusting of the senses. In his dialogue *The Republic*, Plato outlines the reasons why he considers sense experience to be 'at third remove from the truth'. By this he means that sense impressions provide us with sometimes illusory information about the world, and can therefore be considered the lowest form of knowledge. As he points out:

> a stick will look bent if you put it in the water, straight when you take it out, and deceptive differences of shading can make the same surface seem to the eye concave or convex; and our minds are clearly liable to all sorts of confusions of this kind. It is this natural weakness of ours that the scene-painter and conjuror and their fellows exploit with magical effect.[12]

Plato (c.427-347 BC)

In other words, our senses are easily fooled, and we cannot base any certain knowledge upon such an insecure foundation (thus, incidentally, Plato banished all artists (scene-painters) from his ideal society (or Republic), since they dealt only in illusion). For Plato, therefore, of the four types of knowledge which he identified, sensory knowledge was the furthest away from truth.

Better than sense experience are the beliefs that we create from them (at two removes – or steps – from truth), because the creation of such beliefs at least involves a degree of conscious reflection. However, these may still sometimes prove incorrect, and therefore ultimately lack knowledge and certainty. Better still is the use of reason to arrive at a critical understanding of our beliefs, where we may *deduce* the truth through logical analysis. However, even this is still one step away from truth itself, because our reason is only as trustworthy as the assumptions on which we base it. Therefore, a system may be logical and consistent while still proving to be false. For example, if we accept the premise that animals are a lower form of life than humans, and can therefore be used as we see fit, then we can 'justify' our actions in a perfectly logical way *as long as we do not question this assumption*. However, Plato implies, all logical reasoning must utilize assumptions which cannot themselves be arrived at through logic, but must simply be 'grasped' or 'apprehended'. Plato therefore proposes that the surest basis of knowledge is to understand truth *directly* by contemplation of the ideas that exist independently of us (which he called the *forms*), examples of which would be 'goodness', 'justice', and 'beauty'. These ideas, he argues, are not to be arrived at (we do not deduce what 'beauty' is), but rather exist already, and provide standards by which we can make judgements (this is similar to Descartes's concept of innate ideas).

Plato's Concept of Knowledge

Understanding	Reason	Belief	Sense Experience
Most pure. Allows us to see things as they really are.	Allows us to arrive at knowledge by deduction and logic.	Judgements based on hearsay, assumptions, others' opinions, etc.	The information which arrives through the senses, accepted at face value.
Knowledge: Only via understanding and reason can we claim to truly know things.		Opinion: Belief and sense experience cannot give us knowledge, only opinion - which may be wrong.	

It may be argued that there are a number of points of agreement between Descartes and Plato. Both philosophers distrust the senses, while both propose that ultimate truth can only be found in the clear apprehension of innate or self-evident truths. Thus, for both, the reason why the senses lead us into error is that they seem to encourage false opinions. Therefore, to rid ourselves of these opinions – and to avoid being misled by sensory illusion – we must question those assumptions upon which the opinions are based.

However, not all philosophers have agreed with the argument from the senses (as it is also called). Firstly, as Marin Mersenne points out in the sixth set of Objections, why do we need to distrust *all* the senses? For instance, Mersenne argues, when we see a stick bent in water

> what corrects the error? The understanding? Not at all; it is the sense of touch.[13]

Descartes's response to this is to ask what reason we have for trusting one sense (touch) over another (sight). To find such a reason, we must use the understanding (and not sense experience).

Some modern philosophers, however, have argued that rather than admit that the errors to which the senses are prone leave us needing to find an absolute truth or guarantee for knowledge, we may instead consider those errors themselves to be in some way informative. So, let us take a typical sceptical example: two people, one coming into a warm room from outside on a cold day, and one who has been in the room for some time. Now, each of them placing their hands into a bowl of water will feel it to be a different temperature (to the person coming in from outside, the water will appear hotter than to the person who has not left the room). So, the sceptic argues, our senses cannot be trusted to provide us with accurate information about the temperature of the water. However, need this be a problem? The fact that different body temperatures make the water seem hotter or colder may be seen to teach us something about our subjective experiences (e.g. that our senses may react differently according to how they have been influenced beforehand). Similarly, if we come into a dark place from a well-lit place, we may see very little, whereas someone whose eyes have been accustomed to the dark, or who has come there from an even darker place, will be able to see better.[14]

Similar counter-arguments can be applied to other sceptical examples. For instance, it may be said that the famous stick-in-water example (mentioned in the earlier quote from Plato) merely shows us that light behaves differently in water than it does in air, and that we must adjust our beliefs accordingly. Optical illusions – such as mirages – tell us facts about perception, human psychology, etc. So, the counter-sceptic argues, rather than considering such examples as evidence of the untrustworthiness of the senses, we should realize that such 'mistakes' are actually *teaching* us about the nature of the world and ourselves.[15]

However, the argument from illusion is not dead, for while this sort of counter-argument is appealing, it does not guarantee that secure knowledge can be achieved. In other words, the sceptic may still argue that, even if the times in which we are mistaken become apparent as we learn more about the world (and ourselves), there is no certain way of knowing *when* we are deceived. So, it may be true that, even when no deception is apparent to us, it is still present somewhere (and we haven't yet found it – or may *never* find it).

This is a point made by Descartes in the 'Objections and Replies'. Here, the French philosopher Pierre Gassendi suggests that the occurrence of errors in judgement to do with sense perception is not necessarily reason enough to distrust *all* such judgements (and that there may be trustworthy sense perceptions). However, Descartes's response to this objection is correct, I think, for he points out to Gassendi that such a belief would be a mere prejudice, because

> you have no reason to think that all the things in which error can reside have been noticed by you, and it could easily be proved that you sometimes are wrong about those things which you accept as certain.[16]

This is a much stronger argument than the original one in that it does not deny that errors form an important part of how we learn about things, but only that we can never know when those errors are actually present (and that therefore, Descartes argues, what we need is a *reason* to trust certain sense perceptions). This, however, leads on to the more potent argument concerning the possibility of being *constantly* deceived – to which I shall now turn.

Dreaming

To say that the senses cannot be trusted is one thing, but to say that we may be constantly in error is quite another. It is one reply to the argument from illusion to say that if our senses always mislead us, then there would be no sense in which we could ever be 'right' or 'wrong' about things. In other words, to be 'wrong' about something, it must at least be possible to be 'right' about it. Or, to put it another way, for a stick to appear straight or bent in water there must at least *be* a stick. As the Austrian philosopher Ludwig Wittgenstein points out:

> Doubting and non-doubting behaviour. There is a first only if there is a second.[17]

In other words, to doubt something we must first accept a lot of other things. To ask, 'Is that chair really there?', we must first accept that I have an image of a chair, that the image is in some way constant over time, that things change in relation to the chair in an orderly and explicable way, etc. Doubt, therefore, would seem to rely on prior belief (this is not, of course, to say that those prior beliefs are necessarily *correct*, but merely that we cannot be mistaken about *everything*).

However, as you know, Descartes's sceptical arguments do not stop with the argument from illusion. Firstly, he imagines the much more drastic possibility that we may, at this very moment, be dreaming. This is based on the possibility that, when dreaming, the things that we experience can seem completely 'real' to us. The non-sceptic may point out here that dreams do not have the sort of coherence that 'real life' has – people pop up out of nowhere, locations change without warning, impossible things happen (flying and floating unaided, etc.). But is this a convincing response? It may depend on how we interpret the dreaming argument: we may take it to mean that it is possible that I am dreaming at this very moment and not know it; on the other hand, we may take the stronger possibility that life itself is a dream, and that everything is one grand illusion. Since this latter possibility is more the sort of ground that the deception argument covers, I will therefore take Descartes to be implying merely the first possibility.

If I am merely asking, 'Am I dreaming now?' then surely my knowledge of what it is to dream comes into it – and I must answer 'no'. My experience of dreams is that they are, retrospectively, less 'real' (for the reasons already given). We may still point out, of course, that we have dreamt in the past that we were awake, or even that we asked ourselves if we were dreaming *in a dream* (and decided negatively). However, when we compare the quality of being awake with that of dreaming, and our current conception of what it is to be awake with our memory of what dreams are like, then the result *feels* conclusive: we are not dreaming. The sceptic can, of course, argue again that our memory is at fault, or that we are deceiving ourselves as to our ability to tell one state from another. However, it is at least true that my experience of being awake *includes* a memory of a less real state (dreaming), while my experience of dreaming seems to possess certain qualities about it that distinguish it from the waking state (of which, in so-called *lucid* dreams, I can become aware and 'wake up' within the dream).[18]

This, ultimately, leads to Descartes's own answer to the dreaming problem. For, as he states at the very end of the *Meditations*,

> our memory can never connect our dreams with one another and with the general course of our lives, as it is in the habit of connecting the things which happen to us when we are awake.[19]

And therefore, unlike the experience of trying to piece together dream events, when we examine the events of the 'real' world we find that

> after having called upon all my senses, my memory and my understanding to examine them, nothing is reported to me by any one of these faculties which conflicts with what is reported to me by the others.[20]

In other words, Descartes is arguing from *coherence*. So, since my understanding of how events should be connected, how beings and objects should behave, my memories of what has happened, etc., do not conflict with one another (i.e. they are *coherent* with one another), then we can safely trust those events as real (whereas dreams are *incoherent* in that they cause the evidence which comes from distinct faculties to *conflict*).

A sceptic can, of course, argue more than this – i.e. that even our waking states are not real – but doing so would seem to require the provision of an additional step to the argument: that is, that we are *constantly* deceived. If the argument is interpreted merely as 'we cannot tell waking from dreaming (but both states exist)', then it is weaker than saying, 'everything is a dream (or illusion)'. Descartes's version of this latter argument utilizes the idea of an evil demon that has the power to make us experience whatever it wishes. This is the most extreme form of scepticism. At least in relation to dreaming Descartes could still conclude that certain things were true, e.g. that there were such things as triangles, number, and – of course – that he himself exists (the *Cogito*). However, the evil demon argument even calls these things into question.

Furthermore, the evil demon argument – as a stronger form of doubt – will also bring into play the need for a greater form of certainty. Descartes's answer to the dreaming argument – that waking states are more coherently connected than dreaming states – is ultimately unsuccessful (or at least it is only a partial answer). As the English philosopher Thomas Hobbes points out in the Objections, there is no reason why the dreamer cannot 'dream that his idea is connected with a long series of past events' (i.e. that there is coherence to his ideas regarding the world experienced in the dream).[21] For, Hobbes continues, either there are conclusive reasons for differentiating the dreaming and waking states, or else some other proof is needed. This proof is, of course, the clear and distinct idea of a non-deceiving deity. Should we conclude then, Hobbes asks, that an atheist cannot tell dreaming from waking? Descartes's reply is interesting. Firstly, he says, even though the dreamer thinks there is coherence, on waking he will realize his mistake. Seemingly, then, he must wait until he wakes up to know that he is not dreaming – but isn't that what he is trying to decide? Descartes's argument would therefore seem to work only in determining that we are not dreaming when we are awake (and not the other way around). However, even in this he may be mistaken – unless he has a realization of God's part in his clear perceptions. For while

> an atheist is able to infer from memory of his past life that he is awake; still he cannot know that this sign is sufficient to give him the certainty that he is not in error, unless he knows that it has been created by a God who does not deceive.[22]

Thus, Descartes does not dismiss the coherence argument, but admits that – by itself – it is insufficient. True knowledge and certainty, then, must rely on the answer to the question, 'Who is responsible for my existence?' God, or an evil demon?

Deception

Deception arguments can take many forms. I mentioned the film *The Matrix* earlier, but any scenario which implies constant, systematic deception may be considered an example of the deception argument. Since this is the most extreme form of scepticism, it is perhaps the hardest to defeat. Unlike the dreaming argument, we cannot appeal to the fact that we know what it is like to be in an undeceived state, *since everything we experience may in fact be part of that deception.* What we are looking for, then, is some *internal* guarantee that our experiences are in some sense real ('internal', that is, to the world of our own experiences – as opposed to relying on the assumption that something exists 'outside' them). Descartes's attempt to do this relies, ultimately, on the existence of God, the fact that He is not a deceiver, the notion of clear and distinct ideas, and the *Cogito*. However, I will consider his arguments for the existence of God and the part that these play in his system later on,[23] so for now I will be concerned solely with the question of whether the absolute certainty which he claims to have found – that while he thinks, he exists – is as 'clearly and distinctly true' as he thinks it is.

The Cogito

In the light of the possibility that he may be the subject of constant deception by an evil demon, Descartes concludes that the one thing he *can* be certain of is that even if what he perceives is false, it is at least true that *he perceives*. After all, he cannot be deceived about the fact that he is having perceptions, because to be deceived about that must necessarily involve some perception or thought, and that would be self-contradictory. He therefore concludes that it is at least true that while he perceives (or thinks), he exists. This famous conclusion has, however, been doubted and criticized from various perspectives.

Among Descartes's contemporaries, criticism took a number of forms. Gassendi, for instance, asked why Descartes had chosen thought as the basis for proving necessary existence. Why, he argued, can't we say, 'I walk, therefore I am'? In this case, however, Gassendi's objection is not that the *Cogito* doesn't prove what it sets out to, but rather that it is too restrictive:

> You might have inferred that from any other activity, since our natural light informs us that whatever acts also exists.[24]

But does our 'natural light' inform us (i.e. is it obvious to us) that 'whatever acts also exists'? In his reply, Descartes argues that it does not, because at this stage of doubt in the second Meditation, the existence of physical things is still uncertain (it may yet prove to be a dream or illusion). Furthermore, only the mind, as the thing we know most intimately and best, is free from this doubt.

But what sort of knowledge does this represent? As Descartes points out, 'I walk, therefore I am' fails because we need to assume the existence of a physical body, that other beings have minds, etc. However, how does Descartes arrive at the conclusion that he is a 'thinking thing'? Doesn't this involve similar assumptions? This is the point made by Mersenne, where he objects that if I say, 'I think, therefore I am', I already have an idea of what 'thinking' is, and what 'existence' involves.[25] However, aren't these the very things that are being investigated? Normally, we would use 'existence' to mean 'having physical form', but Descartes has already cast doubt on that possibility, so what does 'existence' mean here? The existence of a soul or some sort of 'incorporeal entity'? But what is that? The point, here, before it gets lost, is that there are a number of assumptions involved in the statement which would in turn seem to require supporting arguments.

Modern commentators have also made similar objections. Firstly, there is some ambiguity involved in the statement itself. Does Descartes mean '*Only* while I am thinking, I exist', or 'To be capable of thought is also to exist'? Both statements have very different consequences. On the one hand, if I can only be sure that I exist while I am thinking, then there would appear to be times when I am not thinking (sleep, unconsciousness, watching *The X-Factor*). However, on the other hand, if we interpret him as saying that to be capable of thought is to exist, then how can he know this? Exist as what? Since at this stage of his doubt he is merely concerned with himself as a 'thinking thing', the nature of his existence is unknown to him. Is he a soul, a body, or both? The fact that he is thinking does not clarify this and therefore his existence may only be a temporary phenomenon. Furthermore, he cannot argue from the general fact that 'thinking things exist' that therefore he exists, because that would be to assume not only that the other beings he sees actually exist, but also that they have mental processes similar to his own. The most that the *Cogito* would seem to be able to prove, therefore, is that while I am having the particular thought that I am at that moment having, then I am having that thought (which is, to say the least, unspectacular).

But can it even prove that? The English philosopher A. J. Ayer has argued that:

> 'I exist' does not follow from 'there is a thought now'. The fact that a thought occurs at a given moment does not entail that any other thought has occurred at any other moment, still less that there has occurred a series of thoughts sufficient to constitute a single self. As [David] Hume conclusively showed, no one event intrinsically points to any other. We infer the existence of events which we are not actually observing, with the help of general principles.[26]

In other words, just observing a thought does not prove that a *self* actually exists. We *assume* as a 'general principle' that the self is responsible for the thought, and that also all the thoughts which 'it' has originate from the same self. But this is not justified by the observation alone. Rather, it points to the fact that the idea of the self, that it is a single thing, that it is in some way the same from moment to moment, etc., is either *assumed* (in which case we are unable to prove it) or *created* (in which case it may be that it is *constructed* in some way – perhaps by the behaviour of individuals towards each other in society). This last possibility represents a more modern philosophical attitude towards the self – and, of course, a more radical and 'scary' one (we would all much rather we had a fixed, indivisible, constant self, I'm sure). However, this latter approach sees the idea of the self as being formed rather in the way that we give personalities to inanimate objects or 'lower' life forms:[27] in other words, we *treat them as if they had a self.* Is this what we do with ourselves (or rather, our *selves*)?[28]

Another of Descartes's contemporaries, Thomas Hobbes, chose a similar target by focusing his objections on Descartes's conclusion that the mind is a non-corporeal entity.[29] Why, he argues, should we conclude from the fact that we think, that this is the activity of a spiritual self? Couldn't it just be the activity of a part of the physical body (whose existence at this point is only doubted)? Descartes's mistake, Hobbes argues, is to give an independent existence to the faculty of thought, much as the old scholastic philosophers used to:

> For it does not seem to be good reasoning to say: I am exercising thought, hence I am thought; or I am using my intellect, hence I am intellect. For in the same way I might say, I am walking; hence I am the walking.[30]

Hobbes's point is an interesting one, for it was common for scholastic philosophers to say things like, 'the understanding understands, the vision sees, will wills', and so on, thus creating independent faculties which were responsible for these particular jobs. Hobbes, however points out that this is a particularly artificial way of talking, and that it is much more natural to say, 'I understand, I see, I will', etc. However, what, then, is this 'I'? Hobbes, who was a materialist, proposes that this self is not incorporeal (as Descartes argued), but rather *corporeal* (i.e. physical), and that therefore all the things we call mental could be accounted for in physical terms (which is largely what modern philosophers of mind believe, the majority of whom are materialists).

The *Cogito*, then, would seem not to prove what Descartes thought it did. The most it seems to prove is that, 'There is a thought, therefore there is a thought' – which is a tautology, and therefore doesn't really tell us anything.[31] Or are we being unfair to Descartes? There are some concepts which are relevant here, but since I consider them in full later, I will only briefly outline their significance for this question. Firstly, we may not see Descartes as necessarily committing himself to there being one, indivisible self (or that the *Cogito* proves this). Rather, it may be argued, one of his primary concerns is in establishing what the true nature of things is. So, in arguing that his true nature lies in thinking, and that he is separate from the body, one of his main concerns is in showing that there exist at least two separate and distinct substances: mental and physical. That this is true can be shown from the distinct properties or attributes which each substance possesses. Thus 'thinking' is simply a *mode* (or modification) of mental substance, while 'occupation of space' (which Descartes called *extension*) is a mode of physical stuff.[32] Obviously, there are particular criticisms of this distinction (which I shall also deal with later), but it perhaps rescues the *Cogito* somewhat if we reconsider its purpose in this way.

Another defence of the argument comes from Descartes himself. Certain critics, Descartes points out, treat the *Cogito* as a *syllogistic* argument. That is, they see it as an argument with two premises and a conclusion, i.e. (P1) I am a thinking thing, (P2) thinking things must exist, therefore (C) I exist. However, this is a misinterpretation. In replies to two of Mersenne's objections,[33] Descartes argues that what is involved in the *Cogito* is not a chain of reasoning, but rather an 'internal cognition',[34] or 'a primitive act of knowledge derived from no syllogistic reasoning'.[35] Thus, when we consider our own nature, it is not only apparent to us that we are thinking things, but also that we exist. This would seem to leave the argument somewhat baseless and open to the criticism of subjectivity (what is 'apparent' to one person is not so to another). However, as we shall see later when we look at foundationalism, the crux of the matter is a deep problem in philosophy, and we must not be overly critical of Descartes for presenting a controversial solution to a still debated topic.

Lastly, before moving on, it is worth considering the question of the status of the *Cogito* itself. If, for example, the malicious demon has the power to undermine the certainty of *any* assertion, or even to make Descartes think that false assertions are true, then why should it yet be that the *Cogito* is true? Here, some commentators have argued, is the main flaw in Descartes's system: If the *Cogito* is 'clearly and distinctly' true, then what guarantees clear and distinct ideas? I shall now explore this very question.

Clear and Distinct Ideas

Descartes's solution to the demon argument contains one other component – that of clear and distinct perception. With this, Descartes attempts to show that certain ideas are what philosophers sometimes call 'self-evident' (that is, that they provide, by their own nature and existence, evidence for their own truth).

But what do these terms actually signify? As I noted in my summary, Descartes considered that ideas could be clear without being distinct: a pain, for instance, is clear to us, but does not give us enough information about its nature, or location, etc.; 'God', however, or the number '3', are distinct *and* clear, in that their nature is apparent to us and they are capable of being well understood by us. However, an idea *cannot* be distinct without first being clear (in other words, if an idea is distinct, it must also be clear). I hope that's clear!

The first problem with this doctrine, however, is that it is vague. Firstly, the idea of clarity seems to imply the force with which an idea impresses itself upon us. So, pain cannot be ignored because it presses upon our awareness, whereas fleeting impressions, half-formed ideas, and confused notions – such as the notion of dragons or four-sided triangles – possess 'less reality'. Descartes talks of things pressing upon us with 'sufficient strength',[36] but what does he mean by this? Perhaps that, if I see a certain mixture of shapes and colours present together in one place, the idea of an object *clearly* presents itself to me, whereas in the chance collection of random elements (such as, perhaps, when a cloud resembles a certain thing), the sense of that object being there is weak and unclear.

But how does this work with numbers, geometrical figures, or abstract concepts? Do these press themselves on my attention in the same way? Descartes's idea here seems to be that people frequently possess clear but *indistinct* ideas about the nature of the world. For instance, everyone has a direct experience of gravity, though they may not understand its principles to any great degree, or even be aware of it *as* gravity. To possess a clear *and* distinct concept of gravity we must therefore analyse our assumptions to do with certain things (e.g. falling apples). To say an apple falls because the branch is no longer holding it does not really tell us much; to say that 'things tend to fall downward' tells us more, but is still very general and vague; but to say that things attract one another, and that therefore objects of smaller mass (apples) are drawn towards objects of greater mass (the earth), is to get pretty close to a clear and distinct understanding of why the apple falls.[37]

However, this seems a rather simple picture of how we acquire knowledge. Why, for instance, in looking at an apple, should it be the idea of gravitation that impresses itself upon me? Why not something else – such as the principles of aerodynamics? Or something to do with the way light produces the red colour? Or, in fact, the idea that 'an apple a day keeps the doctor away'? These are all ideas that may spring from the experience of seeing the apple fall, and there would seem to be no guarantee – or reason – that one particular idea should *clearly* impress itself upon me. What, then, is being clearly impressed upon us?

Perhaps, however, this is being unfair to Descartes. If you recall, a similar point was discussed in relation to the ontological argument when Descartes anticipated the objection that, even if it were true that whenever we consider the idea of God we must conclude that He necessarily exists, it is not necessary that we ever actually think of Him.[38] Descartes's response there was to say that even if we were not automatically led to think of the idea of God, if ever we were to think of a being greater than ourselves, or of a greatest being, we *must* accordingly give Him certain features and properties (such as omniscience, omnipotence, etc.). Descartes's point would therefore seem to be not that we *must* think of certain ideas (such as God, or the law of gravity), but rather that when we come to think of certain things (such as a being greater than ourselves, or why the apple falls), certain concepts or explanations seem to be more logically coherent than others. However, even allowing for this, I would still suggest that the very notion of 'clarity' is not as easily defined as Descartes might hope (I shall return to this in the next section, 'Scientific Knowledge').

As regards distinctness, Descartes points to mathematical concepts and the idea of God as prime examples. These ideas are distinct, he says, inasmuch as they can be conceived of without confusion or imprecision. The number '3' therefore is more distinct than the experience of having toothache because the impression of the latter leaves us unsure as to where it is, what causes it, etc., whereas the former can be shown to be consistent and fully understood in all its operations. This may, in a way, be true, but is it true for the reasons Descartes thinks? Our knowledge of pain is indistinct when it is based solely on subjective experience (what I immediately feel), whereas if I seek an *objective* view of the pain (by visiting a doctor, submitting to tests, scans, etc.), then the knowledge can be distinct. However, my knowledge of the number '3' is not a parallel case (most modern philosophers would agree). Pain is related to a physical object (my body), whereas the concept of the number '3' is, strictly speaking, not an object in any sense.[39] It may be argued that we do not 'get to know' the number '3' in the same way that we understand pain. Knowing how the concept '3' should be understood is more like knowing how to make a move in a particular game, whereas knowing what pain signifies is about knowing how the body works, how it relates to subjective experience, etc.[40]

These criticisms aside, there is one objection to clear and distinct ideas which presents a greater problem. In short, how do we know that clear and distinct ideas guarantee knowledge? Leaving the evil demon argument aside for a moment, what is there about an idea being clear and distinct which suggests that it must be true? It seems to me that Descartes is caught between wanting to say something like 'we must rely on our innate sense of knowing when something is true', and wanting to find a guarantee for something being true.[41] For instance, when you consider whether it is true that you are sitting reading this book, what tells you that the idea you have is true? Is it true because it is 'clear and distinct', or would you say that 'it just *is* true'? The problem is that philosophy is primarily the search for reasons. The very idea that we can prove one thing or justify another is based on the practice of supplying reasons why it is true. But when we ask ourselves why things which we consider true are true, we find ourselves looking for reasons why the reasons we use to justify things are justified. If that last sentence sounds confusing, then that's just as it should be, because the whole process leads us infinitely backward. For any reason we find must in turn be backed up by another reason, and so on to infinity.

What Descartes has highlighted here – though not intentionally – has become a central problem of philosophy. Descartes's failure in this respect is therefore useful: we know that if we are to seek to guarantee knowledge, we must go about it another way. Descartes's own solution to the dilemma is, of course, that we just *are* sure, and the only way we can doubt that self-assurance is if the evil demon argument is actually true.[42] Descartes's solution therefore rests on whether he can actually prove that God is not a deceiver – a question which in turn leads to the problem of the so-called Cartesian Circle (which I deal with in a later section).

Scientific Knowledge

One final problem with the doctrine of clear and distinct ideas is the role that Descartes envisaged it playing in our search for scientific knowledge of the physical world. Earlier, we considered two examples of ways in which the notion of clear and distinct ideas might help us towards knowledge. One of these, the idea of God, was held up by Descartes as a template of ideas which are most clear and distinct. However, the other example I considered – that of gravity – provides an interesting application of Descartes's method.

Firstly, it should be noted that Descartes was critical of much contemporary scientific method. For example, in relation to the scholastic view of gravitation, he states that

> although experience shows us very clearly that the bodies we call 'heavy' descend towards the centre of earth, we do not for all that have any knowledge of the nature of what is called 'gravity' – that is to say, the cause or principle which makes bodies descend in this way.[43]

Thus, explanations of gravity which simply stated that things fell 'because they were heavy' (which is essentially what scholastic philosophy proposed) were ultimately unenlightening because 'heaviness' itself was left unexplained. Descartes's proposal, therefore, was to attempt to reduce all such phenomena to explanations which could ultimately be traced back to the clear and distinct, absolutely certain, first principles which Descartes's philosophical method was designed to uncover.

However, in practice, Descartes himself did not appear to follow his own rules. For example, in an account of how we see light and colour, Descartes proposed that differences in colour occurred because of the different speeds of rotation of the infinitely small particles that made up the world. Thus, a slower motion produces a blue colour, while a faster motion produces a red one. Now, apart from being simply wrong, Descartes's theory does not seem to be deduced from any first principle. As Derek Gjertsen points out

> Whether light particles rotated or not was something Descartes could neither deduce from first principles nor observe. His selection of this property [i.e. the spinning of particles] was as arbitrary as the effect he assigned to it [i.e. the variance in colour due to speed of rotation]. On numerous other occasions he described equally arbitrary mechanisms to account for the familiar phenomena of nature.[44]

In other words, if the details of Descartes's theory are simply chosen at will (arbitrarily), and cannot have been deduced directly from first principles, then what is there to guarantee the theory's certainty? The answer to this is simply that such accounts (e.g. of how light works) are *hypotheses* which may or may not be true. However, Descartes argued, we may judge the accuracy of these accounts by their explanatory power. So, if my theory of light also accounts for magnetism, fire, and other natural phenomena, for instance, then it is more likely to be true. Of course, while this is in a sense true, it does not hide the fact that Descartes's method does not differ as radically from the scholastic one as one might first suppose. Both are what might be called *a priori* methods in that they attempt to argue from things which are held to be absolutely certain and true (so called, *first principles*). Therefore, the only difference would appear to be the things that the two approaches would consider to be certain first principles. Descartes's main criticism of scholasticism, therefore, was that it based its conclusions about the world on false first principles, whereas the criticism of a modern scientist would be that it did not base its conclusions on actual observation and experiment – an allegation which we can now see can be equally levelled at Descartes himself.

One final point regarding these first principles is how they should be applied. For instance, if we have two competing theories, on what grounds should we prefer one over another? Via its coherence with other theories? What if those other theories are wrong? Should we choose the simpler theory?[45] But why should nature follow the simpler course? Descartes's method would therefore seem to be open to this sort of mistake by pursuing a purely theoretical approach. As the nineteenth-century Scottish philosopher Thomas Reid pointed out, theorizing from the comfort of your own armchair is not the best way to gain scientific understanding of the world:

> If a 1000 of the greatest wits that ever the world produced were, without any previous knowledge of anatomy, to sit down and contrive now, and by what internal organs, the various functions of the human body are carried on . . . they would not in 1000 years, hit upon anything like the truth.[46]

Dualism

Substance

Descartes is most commonly described as a dualist. This is the belief that the world consists of two types of *substance*: mental stuff and physical stuff.[47] The philosophical idea of substance is an old one and goes back to the philosophy of Aristotle, who considered a substance to be that which possessed properties, but which was not itself a property. For instance, a dog can be brown, and thus we can say that the dog (the substance) possesses the property of 'being brown' or 'brownness'. Properties cannot exist on their own (*something* must be brown), and therefore cannot themselves be considered substances; on the other hand, substances cannot be the properties of other things (so, a cat can be 'brown', but it cannot be 'dog').[48]

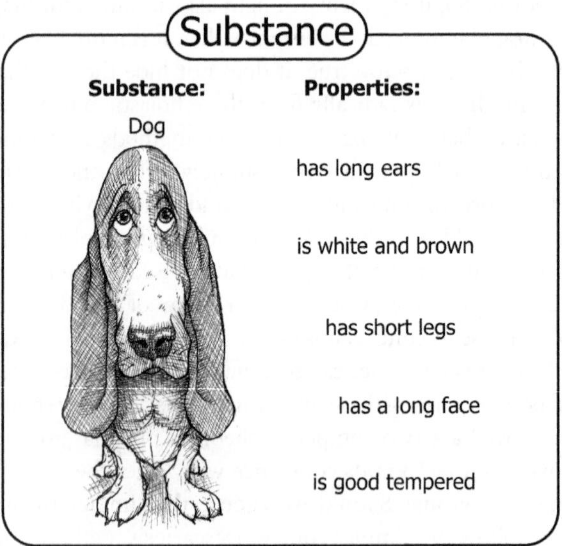

A substance is that which possesses properties (or qualities), but is not itself a property.

Mind and Matter

Mind	*Matter*
Conscious, sentient, intelligent, etc.	Not capable of thought, feeling, or intelligence
Without shape, size, weight, and not located in space	Possessing shape, size, weight, and located in space
Indivisible, immeasurable	Divisible, measurable

The search for the substance or substances which underlie the properties we come across is therefore a search for the real nature of the world, and an attempt to answer the question of what it is made of. Thus, for Descartes, there were two *types* of substance, of which each individual mind or physical object was an example. However, for Spinoza, there was only one substance, of which mind and matter were merely *modifications* (or modes).[49] Leibniz, in contrast to both of these, proposed that there were an infinite number of substances (or *monads*, as he called them), of which each mind (or soul) was an instance.[50]

Descartes's division of the world into two, as we have seen, stems from an examination of his own nature (he is a thinking thing), and that which he is not – or, more precisely, not *essentially* (i.e. his physical body). He does not deny that his body belongs to him, but only rejects the idea that it is essential to his being (just as I might exist without a limb and still be the same person, so, he argues, 'I' can exist without my body and still be 'me').

Descartes then goes on to set up an opposition which has caused subsequent philosophers no end of problems. It looks something like this:
So, mind is a thinking thing (or, as Descartes calls it in Latin, *res cogitans*), but without dimension or physical existence. On the other hand, matter is *res extensa* (Latin: an 'extended thing' – that is, it extends itself in different directions – length, breadth, height). You will notice that, apart from being conscious, sentient, etc., the other qualities possessed by mind are negative versions of those possessed by matter. We can see, touch, weigh, measure, etc., most physical things, but the mind – or mental stuff – is defined in part by our *inability* to do those things. This is a bit frustrating for anyone trying to get to

grips with Descartes's concept of mind. In one sense, of course, there is no problem: we all are familiar with our own mind, and know what it is to be conscious (even if we cannot necessarily define what exactly our mind *is* or what being conscious actually *involves*). However, there is also a sense in which the nature of the mind remains essentially mysterious, even mystical.

One of the problems for Descartes's concept of mind is therefore that it is almost as if it has been defined as the *opposite* of matter – not that Descartes would have expressly intended this. However, many philosophers (e.g. Gilbert Ryle) have pointed out that talking about mind as any sort of substance at all is misleading in that in doing so we would seem to be treating it *as if* it were physical (I explore Ryle's position in more detail below).

Regarding Cartesian dualism more generally, there are two main problems which are traditionally identified:

1. I seem to be aware of controlling my body via my thoughts, and I also seem to receive messages (or *natural teachings*) from it in terms of sensations, pains, etc. Yet, if the two substances are so different in almost every way, how do they interact?
2. If we can't interact with or detect mental substance *in any way*, how do we know that it exists? Mightn't it be better to account for the mind in terms that we *can* measure? That is, by looking at how the physical substance of the brain produces and enables conscious thought?

Interactionism

The first problem has become known as the *problem of interaction*, and Descartes's picture of what mind and body are and how they relate to each other, *Interactionism*. The problem itself can be put quite simply: how can a physical and a non-physical thing interact? If I want to move something – a pen on my desk, for example – it may begin with an 'immaterial' thought (the desire to move the pen), but actually to move it I must have some physical means (e.g. my hand). Now, if the body is to be affected, surely it must have a physical cause. Think about it: the body is not intelligent in the sense that we can communicate with it and hope it understands; however, neither, for Descartes, can my thought *cause* the physical nerves, tendons, and muscles to reach for the pen. Of course, a nerve can stimulate a muscle, and a muscle can move another muscle, but these cause-and-effect relationships are all physical. This is known as a 'causally closed system'.[51] Physical things act on physical things and, of course, mental things act on mental things (one thought leads to another). But both 'systems' seem closed to outside influences, and therefore each other.

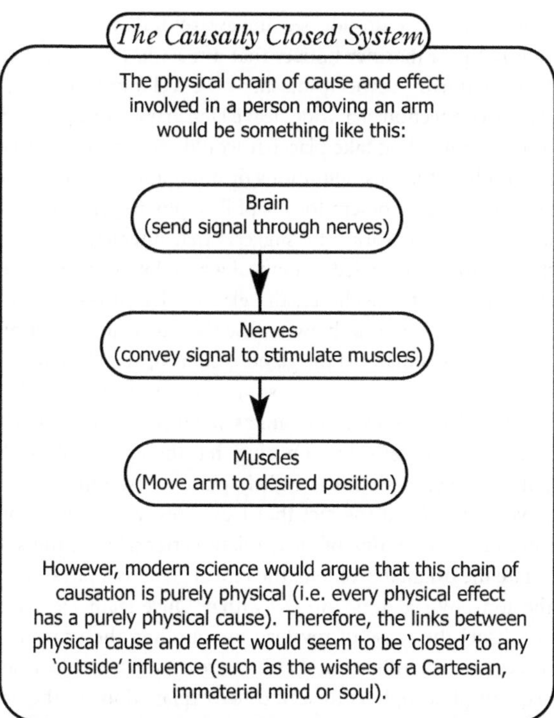

The Causally Closed System
The physical chain of cause and effect involved in a person moving an arm would be something like this:
Brain (send signal through nerves)
Nerves (convey signal to stimulate muscles)
Muscles (Move arm to desired position)
However, modern science would argue that this chain of causation is purely physical (i.e. every physical effect has a purely physical cause). Therefore, the links between physical cause and effect would seem to be 'closed' to any 'outside' influence (such as the wishes of a Cartesian, immaterial mind or soul).

Similar points were made by some of Descartes's contemporaries, notably Pierre Gassendi,[52] who wondered 'how the corporeal can have anything in common with the incorporeal'.[53]

Descartes has two main responses to this. The first of these is what has come to be called the *intermingling thesis*, in which – you may recall – he argues that:

> I am not only lodged in my body, like a pilot in his ship, but [. . .] am joined to it very closely and indeed so compounded and intermingled with my body, that I form, as it were, a single whole with it.[54]

This would seem to undermine somewhat the distinctions he has already made between the two types of substances. However, I think that what is really happening here is that Descartes is sincerely trying to account for the differences between mind and body, while also trying to be true to his own experience. He knows that we do not receive messages from our body as if we were piloting a

(*Continued*)

ship (or driving a car); we do not become aware of damage to it, for instance, in the same way that a mariner notices that a mast has become damaged (or a driver that a wing mirror has been smashed): we feel it immediately, which suggests a very close connection. This does leave Descartes with a problem, however: how does this intermingling take place? It would seem that either he must give up the idea, or admit that his definitions of mind and body need to be revised (which would be a huge problem for his philosophy in general).

Elsewhere, in another work,[55] he suggests that interaction might take place via a structure in the brain called the pineal gland. Situated in the centre of the brain between the two hemispheres, the gland – Descartes argues – is ideally placed to act as a meeting point between the two substances. Part of the reason for his suggesting this is that, (a) the gland is central, and (b) it does not appear in animals (thus suggesting that it is in some way associated with the possession of 'reason' – which Descartes saw humans as having and animals not). Of course, Descartes is not here necessarily proposing that the gland 'solves' the problem of interaction, but merely that it is a likely place where interaction might take place. However, apart from the fact that Descartes was wrong about (b) (it is also to be found in the brains of all craniate vertebrates[56]), the solution only seems to restate the original problem: the pineal gland is a physical structure, so how does the non-physical mind interact with it? Once again, Descartes's account does little to dispel the sense of mystery surrounding the problem, and while this is not necessarily an indication that it is wrong, it nonetheless has motivated many subsequent philosophers to seek other explanations of the nature of the mind and its relationship to the body.

It might not be fair, however, to consider these – arguably unsuccessful arguments – as indications of the failure of dualism itself. Furthermore, Descartes himself did not believe that the problem of interaction was itself an insurmountable difficulty. The reason for this is that, firstly, his purpose in the *Meditations* was not necessarily to present solutions to these difficulties, but merely to establish that mind and body were indeed separate and distinct substances. For, he points out in a reply to Gassendi, 'the explanation of the nature of the union between soul and body [is] a matter of which I have not yet treated.'[57] In other words, he is not here presenting an explanation of how interaction takes place, but merely noting that the substances are distinct (and that, therefore, he cannot be criticized for not overcoming these difficulties). Furthermore, he points out,[58] Gassendi has assumed that mind and matter must interact as physical objects do (by influencing each other by contact). However, this cannot happen with two such separate substances, and therefore there must be some other means of influence (which, admittedly, Descartes does not yet understand, but has not – unlike Gassendi – ruled out).

Descartes therefore rejects all criticism of the problem of interaction, because he is convinced that dualism is correct (and therefore that he is only to be judged on the success of his arguments for it). In this sense, therefore, he is like someone who is witness to an unexplained phenomenon (seeing a ghost, for instance). Instead of rejecting the phenomenon (so that we can retain our traditional understanding of the world), he stands by it, even though no current understanding can account for it.

The Arguments

Given all the problems that Cartesian dualism faces, are there any good reasons for accepting it? What are Descartes's arguments for establishing the distinction in the first place?[59] The first of these has become known as the *conceivability argument*, which argues that it is possible to conceive of the mind as having a potentially separate existence from the body. The existence of the body, along with that of the material world, can be doubted, while the existence of the mind cannot. However, as many commentators have pointed out, just because we can or cannot conceive of something being the case does not necessarily decide the truth of the matter (for instance, a child who has never seen snow might not be able to conceive of it, but that has no bearing on its possible or actual existence).

Antoine Arnauld, a contemporary of Descartes, also pointed out that it is perfectly possible to conceive of something clearly while also being ignorant of other properties that it possesses. So, for example, we might think of certain properties of a triangle (e.g. that it has 3 sides), and be ignorant of others (e.g. that the internal angles must equal 180 degrees). Similarly, then, we might conceive of certain properties of the mind (e.g. that it is a thinking thing), and be ignorant of others (e.g. that it is reliant upon the body for its existence).[60] Furthermore, both Johannes Caterus[61] and Arnauld[62] criticized Descartes's attempt to argue from the mere possibility of conceivability to actual separate existence. Arnauld points out that all Descartes is really doing is *abstracting* certain properties and crediting them with an independent existence, which in fact they do not have. So, he argues, while we can talk about 'length' or 'height' in abstract terms, in reality, these things cannot exist separately from the things which possess them (the objects which *are* a certain 'length' and 'height'). Thus, just because we can conceive of the mind abstractly, this does not mean that it has separate existence.

(*Continued*)

Descartes's response to this is to distinguish between essential and inessential properties of an idea. So, he says, we cannot imagine a triangle which did not have 3 sides (it would not be a triangle), but we can imagine a body without a mind, and therefore mind is inessential to body. But is body inessential to mind? Descartes claims that it is because we can conceive of the mind as not possessing any physical properties. But is this really the same as saying that mind is not dependent on the body? There may be some confusion here between the role of subjective experience (being a mind), and that of objective existence (having a mind). Obviously, being a mind is nothing like being an inanimate physical object (though it's difficult to know!). However, this is not to say that *having a mind* is not, in some way, dependent on physical existence. However, the problem is a deep one, and runs right through modern philosophy of mind.

Secondly, Descartes argues that the mind and body are obviously of distinct natures, because the latter is divisible, whereas the former isn't (this is called the *divisibility* or *spatial argument*). So, since the mind has no physical properties and yet exists, then it must have a separate form of non-material existence. However, there are again problems with this argument. On the one hand, modern research into the brain has called this assumption into question. For instance, experiments involving 'split brain' patients, who – in an attempted cure for life-threatening, epileptic seizures – have had the bridge (the *corpus callosum*) linking the two sides of the brain (or *hemispheres*) severed, have provided some remarkable and startling results.[63] Such experiments have suggested that while consciousness *appears* to be unified, there can in fact be occasions when damage to specific sections of the brain causes different parts of it to work independently– but intelligently – for different purposes.

For instance, in a series of well-known experiments, a number of 'split-brain' patients were asked to identify pictures of items that were flashed before them on a screen. In one case, an image of a cup was shown so that it only appeared to the right eye, and an image of a spoon was shown so that it only appeared to the left eye, resulting in different responses.[64] So, when asked what she saw, the patient responded verbally by saying 'cup', but when asked to identify the object by touch alone with the left hand (the one linked to the right hemisphere), she identified the spoon. This is because the one eye will pass information to one side of the brain (for instance, the side where the potential for speech is located in most people), while the other eye will pass information to the other side (the 'speechless' side). Furthermore, since there is no longer any possibility of communication between the two hemispheres,

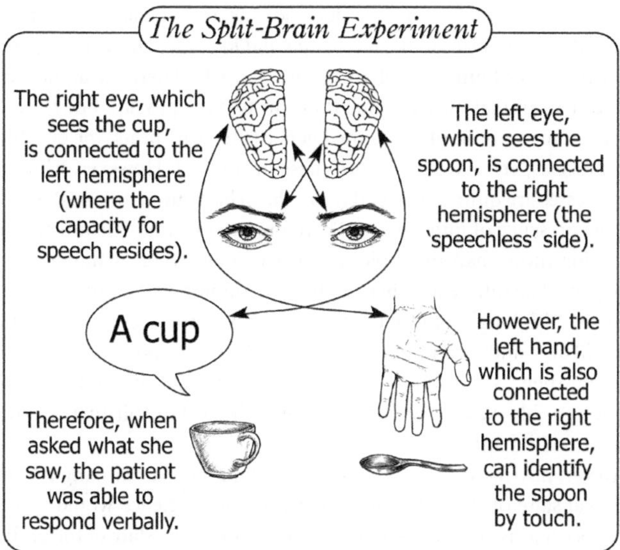

the bridge between them having been severed, there is no way for the brain to 'cross-check' the information it has received through each eye (as it normally would). This is a very strange situation, and can be very upsetting for the patient (who is frequently surprised after having identified the object communicated to the 'speechless' hemisphere, because there is no awareness of having seen that image).

Furthermore, while such findings call into question Descartes's assertion that the brain is indivisible, one may argue that *indivisibility* is itself no guarantee of *separability*. For instance, as John Cottingham points out, even if the mind *were* indivisible, this is not to say that it is not an 'indivisible *property* of an extended thing (for example, the brain)'.[65] In this way, the mind might not be distinct from the physical brain at all (in the way that Descartes hopes it is).

This point was also made by Arnauld: 'the power of thinking seems to be attached to corporeal organs', he says, 'because we can believe it to be asleep in infants, extinguished in the case of lunatics'.[66] In other words, the state of the physical brain, if it is undeveloped or damaged, seems to affect our ability to think. Interestingly, however, Descartes's response does not reject Arnauld's point, but only qualifies it. There is obviously, he says, a close connection

(*Continued*)

between mind and brain, but this does not mean that the two are not in fact separate. At another place in the *Objections and Replies*,[67] Descartes explains what similarities he sees humans as sharing with animals. There, he argues that both have so-called 'animal spirits' which flow through the physical body and provide it with a certain amount of basic intelligence (the heart beats, the eyes blink, the stomach digests, etc. – we might call these 'instincts'). However, while at times these processes are quite developed (as in the behaviour of animals), they do not signify the presence of intelligence. Therefore, we must not assume that animals are anything more than mere biological machines, whereas humans possess a rational soul. The difference, then, is that the 'thinking' of animals is automatic, whereas the 'thinking' of humans (the instinctive processes aside) is an expression of will and understanding (which animals do not possess). The essence of the human, then, is to think. (Incidentally, the animal spirits do not solve the interaction problem either, as they are either physical or spiritual, and therefore face the same difficulties.)

However, if Arnauld is right, and the actual process of thinking is affected by the physical state of the brain (with which modern science would agree), then Descartes's response would seem to be inadequate. If the state of the brain affects thinking, then this would seem to suggest that it is *necessary* for thinking. However, this causes a problem for Descartes's view that we are, essentially, incorporeal 'thinking things', because the process of thinking would seem to be tied in to the state of the physical brain. Of course, there are other possibilities: perhaps the physical brain is only necessary to 'train' the mind, or to 'channel' it? However, if we are to be 'thinking things', it needs to be shown that the physical brain is in some way inessential to the thinking process.[68]

The Ghost in the Machine

Partly because of the problem of interaction, and partly because of the problem of conceiving of immaterial substance (and the religious connotations which this involves), most modern philosophers have rejected Cartesian dualism. The English philosopher Gilbert Ryle (1900–76) was especially critical of Descartes, holding him responsible for originating the problem. Ryle termed Cartesian dualism, 'the dogma of the Ghost in the Machine', and argued that it treated mental things as if they were physical (talking of 'substances' and 'interaction', etc.).[69] Even among Descartes's contemporaries, however, there were criticisms of it, and various philosophers proposed alternatives to it. Nicolas Malebranche (1638–1715), who is often considered a Cartesian (though he diverged from Descartes on a number of points), suggested that all things are in fact caused or facilitated by God (a theory known as *Occasionalism*), and that therefore all physical and mental events are 'occasions' at which God exercises his power.[70]

Spinoza, on the other hand, pointed out what may be termed an *asymmetry* in Cartesian dualism, for while matter seems to be one, universal substance (of which single things are a modification), each individual mind is a separate instance of mental substance.[71] He therefore proposed that to even up – or make symmetrical – the definitions of the two substances, mind and body should be considered as really only modifications of the one true substance. This meant ultimately that all 'interaction' was actually somewhat illusory, since there *were* no two separate substances between which interaction could take place (this type of approach is generally known as *double aspect theory*). However, while this solution was favoured by Spinoza (in effect, a type of 'mystical monism'), and many philosophers were reluctant to follow him, some recognized the problem that he had highlighted, which was essentially that Cartesian dualism did not seem to allow for the existence of individual minds. The reason for this is that while physical substance is divisible (allowing for separate objects to exist), there seemed to be no means of distinguishing between different instances of mental substance (between 'you' and 'me'), because mental stuff was *indivisible* and *immeasurable* (meaning it had no boundaries).[72] Leibniz's solution to this was to propose that the universe is made of an infinite amount of substances (which he called *monads*), of which *each individual soul* was a different *type*. Therefore, those things which we consider separate individuals ('your mind', 'my mind', or even 'this tree' and 'that tree') are actually different types of substances. So, whereas Descartes is a dualist, and Spinoza a monist, Leibniz may be considered a *pluralist*. However, while this would seem to allow Leibniz a way out of the interaction problem, he seems not to have taken it, considering the soul immaterial in a largely Cartesian sense. His solution was, instead, that each monad (or substance) was arranged in what he called a *pre-established harmony*, so that everything progresses according to a divine preordained plan. Therefore, no interaction between any of the various substances is in fact necessary, and their actions progress like a giant clockwork mechanism (which, however, raises its own problems to do with free will).[73]

In a way, therefore, while the above theories may in a sense be seen as trying to maintain those aspects of Descartes's dualism which the advocates of each theory thought important, each approach suffers from its own problems.[74] Eventually, then, the majority of subsequent philosophers have decided that the best approach to the mind–body problem is simply to reject the division altogether. This can be done in two ways: we simply reject the whole idea of there being non-physical aspects of mind; or, we reject dualism, but try to retain some sense that 'being conscious' is very different from 'being a chair' (or some other purely physical object).

The first of these alternatives is called *materialism*, and there are many varieties of it. Basically, philosophers who adopt this route try to show that we can account for the mind in purely physical (or *material*) terms. Various attempts have involved trying to reduce talk of mental events to 'dispositions' or possible behaviour (*logical behaviourism*), accounting for the mind in terms of physical brain activity (called *mind–brain identity theory*), and even trying to eliminate the actual ways of speaking in which the problematic notions of an immaterial self actually appear (called, naturally, *eliminativism*).

However, these theories in turn have given rise to criticism from other philosophers who claim that attempting to account for the mental in purely physical terms 'leaves something out'. In other words, describing the physical aspects of being a human being does not tell you what it is like to *be* that person. Therefore, to reduce a human being to just those physical aspects is to leave out the reality of subjective, conscious experience (which is the thing, arguably, which differentiates mental phenomena from purely physical, non-conscious things in the first place).[75] The challenge for these philosophers, therefore, is to make subjective experience a real thing without falling back into the pitfalls of Cartesian dualism.

The Existence of God

Introduction

As we have seen, the existence and nature of God plays a big part in Descartes's search for certainty. I shall deal later with some of the problems to which this gives rise,[76] but for now I want to examine Descartes's arguments for God's existence themselves. The two main arguments which he presents have come to be known as the *trademark argument* and the *ontological argument*.

The Trademark Argument

Descartes argues that he has a true idea of God which can only have come from God Himself; therefore, God must exist (in order to have given him this idea). This, in a nutshell, is the so-called *trademark argument*. In other words, just as you will probably find the name of the company written somewhere on any product you may buy, so are our minds 'inscribed' with the idea of God.

Descartes's argument can be broken down into four main steps:

1. I have an idea of God.
2. I cannot have created this idea myself.

3. An effect must have as much reality as its cause (remember the bullet hole analogy?).
4. The existence of the idea of God therefore suggests the existence of an actual God.

Is this a convincing argument? Firstly, one might question whether Descartes did indeed have a clear idea of God, and if he did not, *how he could know*. The problem here lies partly in the notion of clear and distinct ideas, which argues that some things can be *self-evident* (i.e. obvious without needing proof). Thus, by looking at the idea of God – he implies – I can see that it is a clear idea. But there is so much room for self-deception here. I might think that I have a clear idea of my mother's face (or even my own), but if someone asks me to describe or draw it, I may miss out a significant detail that I hadn't noticed before. However, with the idea of God, what is there even potentially to show that I am wrong? There is God, of course, but then this is not meant to be an argument from religious experience, but a proof of God based on the *idea* that we have of Him.

The objection here is therefore that, if there is no way of checking whether I have a clear concept of God, how can I know that I had not created the idea myself? You might argue that, if I *did* have a true idea of God, then I *would have been unable* to create it myself. However, as I have argued above, it is not necessarily the case that I *do* have a clear idea. Furthermore, Descartes argues that I cannot myself create an idea of an infinite being. But is this true? He rejects the idea that I can simply take a finite thing and imagine it continuing forever (as we might continually add one more step to a journey, or grain of sand to a pile, for example), because this will still only result in a finite thing (only ever increasing by one), and not true infinity. But what is our idea of infinity? Don't we explain the concept to children by using just such examples? Furthermore, we could argue against Descartes that it may be impossible to have an idea of infinity *other than* in this way. What would it consist of? We may think of ideas as pictures, or even in terms of pure concepts (such as in mathematics), but either way we seem to be using finite things (pictures, symbols) in order to suggest infinity. Furthermore, we do not actually need an infinite thing in order to suggest infinity. Think of a picture of a man holding another picture, which in turn is a picture of the same man holding another picture, which in turn . . . and so on.

This obviously has to stop somewhere, but we can at least maintain the illusion to the point at which our unaided eyesight cannot tell where it stops. In this way, however, we would seem to have created the idea of infinity by finite means. It is not *actually* infinity (it stops somewhere), but it doesn't need

to be (it is a symbol). If we can create such an idea, then it would seem to undermine Descartes's arguments, wouldn't it? This discussion can actually be widened out into a more general debate concerning *nativism*, or the view that we are born with certain ideas and capacities – such as the ability to learn language – that are from birth already 'written into' the brain, encoded in our genes, or are 'native' to us by some other means.

Both Hobbes and Mersenne attack the trademark argument in regard to the nature of the idea of God which Descartes claims to have. Firstly, Mersenne[77] points out that, while Descartes rejects the possibility that he can have arrived at the idea of God through some other means (and not received it from God), there are still good reasons for entertaining other possibilities. Perhaps, he argues, we may have received it from our parents, or our education and upbringing? For, natives of various countries do not seem to possess the idea. Furthermore, the idea of perfection could easily have come from our experience of physical perfection in the world. He also points out that it is possible, in this way, to construct ideas that have no actual existence (that is, just because certain physical things seem to be almost perfect, does not mean that there exists a *most* perfect thing).

Descartes responds that even if the idea of God *had* come from his parents' teachings or general education, this still begs the question of how the idea originated. As regards the ideas of infinity or perfection, these cannot be said to have originated in the physical world, because we do not have an image of them. For instance, while we realize through counting that such a process can go on forever, there is no 'infinite number' to which we can point and say, 'that embodies infinity'. Rather, what we have are certain finite things which *suggest* the idea. In a similar way, therefore, aspects of the physical world may *suggest* infinity or perfection, but they cannot be said to give rise to the ideas (in fact, it is only because such ideas exist that they *can* be suggested). The idea we have of God is therefore an 'act of the understanding alone', and thus does not involve images.

Descartes expands upon this latter point in response to Hobbes, who objects that it is impossible to have an idea of God since He is inconceivable.[78] Here we get to the crux of the disagreement between the two philosophers that runs through much of their correspondence: as an empiricist, Hobbes wants to argue that ideas *only* consist of images or sensible forms, whereas Descartes wants to claim that there are such things as pure ideas (which contain no images or other sensory information). This is an important assertion for Descartes, and it is vital that he can prove that he can directly perceive certain ideas (such as that he exists, that he is a thinking thing, that God exists, etc.), otherwise many of his arguments fail. In response to Hobbes, therefore, he argues that we can have a direct perception of the idea of God, which, while it is not 'complete' (for we are finite beings), is nonetheless adequate to inform us of His existence.

The remaining two stages of the trademark argument are also relevant to the discussion of Descartes's ontological argument, so I will consider them together.

The Ontological Argument

Both the trademark argument and the ontological argument concern the idea we have of God. In the trademark argument, we find the idea in our mind and ask how it got there. However, in the ontological argument, it is the content of the idea itself which concerns us. The steps of the argument go something like this:

1. The idea I have of God is of a perfect being.
2. If such an idea did not actually correspond to an existing being (i.e. God), then the idea would contain an imperfection (i.e. God would not exist).

3. Therefore, the idea of a perfect being must also entail the existence of that perfect being.
4. Therefore, the perfect being – God – actually exists.

To begin with, regarding the second step of this argument, it is dubious whether existence can actually be treated in this way. The German philosopher Immanuel Kant (1724–1804) criticized the argument by stating that 'existence is not a predicate'.[79] By this he meant that, while we might say that a certain thing possesses certain qualities (or *predicates*, to use a logical term), whether or not that thing exists is not a quality that it possesses. So, a dog may possess the properties of 'brownness', 'long-hairedness', 'fondness for postmen', but you would not add to that list, 'existence'. Rather, we have an idea of something which does or does not correspond to reality (i.e. that such a dog does, or does not, exist).

Pierre Gassendi makes a similar objection to this.[80] Like Kant, he points out that 'existence' is not a property, and that it is more correct to talk of whether an idea actually corresponds to reality (i.e. whether it exists). To illustrate this, he criticizes Descartes's comparison of the properties of a triangle and God: he says that Descartes is wrong to say that 'existence' is an essential property of the idea of God in the same way that 'having 3 angles' is an essential property of a triangle. Rather, he argues, the equivalent essential properties of God are such qualities as 'omnipotence', 'omniscience', etc., and that we may look at both ideas ('God', 'a triangle') and decide whether such a thing actually exists. In this way, therefore, Gassendi claims that the ontological argument fails.

Descartes's response to this is to point out that existence means different things for triangles and God. With triangles, we may separate their existence from their essence, but with God, we cannot (He is the only being whose existence is *necessary* in this way). As such, then, the idea of God is a special case, and while Gassendi's point would be relevant to the existence of all other things, with God it is not.

A criticism of the third point concerns the question of whether or not we can argue from an idea to reality. This, also, is a central concern of the trademark argument. There, Descartes argued that an effect must have 'as much reality' as its cause. However, arguing from effect to cause as a method of proof has been criticized by the Scottish philosopher David Hume (1711–76), who pointed out that it is impossible in some situations to know conclusively the nature of the thing which acted as the cause.[81] In other words, deciding what gun caused a certain bullet hole is only possible when we are familiar with the range of guns that might do the job – and then we might still be wrong. In relation to God, even if we agree with Descartes that there must be as much reality in the effect as in the cause, we do not necessarily know what that might mean. Say, for instance, that we have been given a false idea of 'God', of 'perfection', or of 'infinity'. In this case, 'possessing as much reality' would only mean 'capable of giving us a false idea'.

This concept of an idea 'possessing more reality' than other ideas was criticized by Hobbes.[82] Doesn't it make more sense, he argued, to say that something either *is* or *isn't* real? Can there really be degrees of reality? In answer to this, Descartes calls upon the distinction between a substance (such as a rock), and its modes (i.e. its relative and subjective properties – such as its colour or texture). Now, the substance has 'more reality' than its modes, because it can be more clearly and distinctly perceived. In a similar way, therefore, the idea of God has more reality than a merely finite human being. The degrees of reality therefore relate to how clearly they can be known. This is very similar to Plato's conception of reality.

So, do both the ontological and the trademark arguments fail? Not necessarily. The nature of religious belief, as the American psychologist and philosopher William James (1842–1910) has pointed out,[83] is that our belief thresholds differ from individual to individual. So, what is 'proof' to one person remains inconclusive to another, and people can hold on to unfashionable beliefs in the face of overwhelming opposition. History has proved 'madmen' to be visionaries, and the majority mistaken. The most that can be said here, I think, is that in terms of being considered unproblematic (as rational proofs for the existence of God), both the ontological and the trademark arguments have their critics.[84]

Rationalism vs. Empiricism

Introduction

Sometimes, looking back at different phases in history, it is tempting and occasionally useful to group together different individuals, theories, etc., under a unifying title. So, in art we talk about *impressionism* or *surrealism*, in politics about *liberalism* and *conservatism*. In doing so, our intention is not so much to imply that these labels are always wholly accurate, but merely to pick out general features for certain purposes (e.g. 'The English are reserved' or 'Americans are extrovert').

It should come as no surprise, therefore, that philosophy also employs such terms. In relation to Descartes and his times, the two movements which are most relevant to our studies are *rationalism* and *empiricism*. *Rationalism* is associated with a number of concepts, but most importantly with the idea that reason is the source of knowledge, and that it is the discovery of rational principles which allows us to make sense of experience.[85] This may be contrasted with the *empiricist* view that experience is the thing which plays the most important role in learning, and that all ideas are formed from information that at one time has come through the senses.

Descartes, along with – for example – Baruch Spinoza, Wilhelm Leibniz, and Plato, may all be considered, in some sense, rationalists. On the other hand, John Locke, Bishop Berkeley, David Hume, and Aristotle, are all commonly thought of as empiricists. However, as I have already suggested, these two titles are only convenient terms, and the individual philosophers, while they shared many ideas in common with their fellow rationalists or empiricists (respectively), also differed on a great many points. It is also worth noting that, while it may be helpful to group these philosophers together in this way, they did not necessarily think of themselves as being of a particular 'school', but merely as philosophers.[86]

This said, we may identify a number of the ideas which we find in Descartes as typically rationalist. However, since it is not my purpose here to undertake a full analysis of rationalism, I will deal only with those few ideas which are relevant to Descartes's arguments in the *Meditations*. Furthermore, in treating of empiricism, I will confine myself to those aspects which provide a direct challenge to the rationalist ideas discussed.

The A Priori *and Necessity*

One of the main differences between the two approaches is the attitude taken to the two main types of knowledge: the *a priori* and the *a posteriori*. The first kind concerns things which we may know prior to, or independently of, experience (*a priori* is a Latin phrase meaning 'that which comes before'). Rationalists and empiricists, however, did not disagree on whether this type of knowledge exists, but merely on what types of things represent *a priori* knowledge, and why. So, for Descartes, this included such things as mathematical and geometrical principles, the idea of God (and other innate ideas: see below), but also truths to do with the real world that could be shown to be *necessary*. This last word has a particular meaning for rationalist philosophy, and concerns things which *must be so*, because they are based on absolutely certain principles. For instance, Descartes held that it was a certain principle that every cause must have an effect, and vice versa. So, when something happens, we can automatically rule out the possibility that it 'came out of nowhere', and conclude that it must *necessarily* have a cause. Thus, while no rationalist would claim that we can decide the nature of the world purely by reflecting on such *first principles*, they would have argued that through such reflection we can know *something* of what the world is like. Furthermore, having discovered such truths at work in the world, we may consider them as being as certain and *necessary* as the truths of mathematics. This would mean that the so-called 'laws of nature' that science is concerned with finding are responsible for a *necessary connection* between events. So, once I am aware that every cause has an effect, and that a drop in temperature to a certain level causes water to freeze, then the fact that water freezes at that temperature is *necessarily true*.[87]

This view that it is possible to uncover the ultimate laws of nature, and that our knowledge of those laws could be certain, stems from the idea that the world is rationally ordered and is capable of being understood by a human intellect. However, some philosophers have disagreed with this approach, and it has been criticized from a number of different directions.

Firstly, it need not be true that the world is rationally ordered. Just because humans possess a certain standard according to which we judge what is true and false, this does not mean that the universe is structured along the same principles. 'Reason' may turn out to be only 'human reason', which may in turn have its limitations.

Secondly, even if the world is rationally ordered, it may not be possible for humans to discover such connections. So, even if there are fixed and necessary laws that govern the universe, we may be forever mistaken about them.[88]

Thirdly, some philosophers – notably Hume – have argued that the idea that we have of a necessary connection between events is actually somewhat of an illusion, and that our knowledge of cause-and-effect relationships comes solely from experience. Hume's argument is based on the observation that when we see one event as the cause of another, it is usually because over time we have formed a 'customary connection in the thought or imagination'[89] between one object or event and another (i.e. we always think of them as appearing together, or one following on from the other). So, when I put my hand near a flame and feel its heat, I conclude that 'fire causes heat'. Furthermore, every occurrence of fire giving off heat that I come across confirms the connection between the two. However, in making that connection, I have not

– Hume argues – discovered anything which is 'necessary', for the understanding I have of it may change. I may discover other things which produce heat, thus falsifying an idea I perhaps had that '*only* fire causes heat'. Because ideas can change in this way, Hume argues, our knowledge of connections is reliant upon experience (since experience may falsify it). Thus, even if there are such things as necessary connections, our knowledge of them will not be certain but rather *contingent* (i.e. subject to possible change or falsification), and may be considered *a posteriori* (from the Latin, 'that which comes after'), since it relies upon experience.[90]

Thus, for Hume and other empiricists, the scope of *a priori* truths was much reduced. Not only did they disagree that the mind held ideas from birth (innate ideas – of which more in a moment), but they also considered the truths of science to be not absolutely certain. Hume considered *a priori* truths to be mere 'relations of ideas',[91] whereby things are 'necessarily so' merely because they are what is called 'true by definition'. So, to use a well-worn example, that 'all bachelors are unmarried' is true merely because *that is what we mean* by the word 'bachelor', i.e. 'an unmarried man'. You don't need to go searching the globe to prove this, for if there is any man who is married, then he is – by definition – not a bachelor.

Another consequence of this view of *a priori* knowledge, however, is that it is tempting to consider such knowledge relative to culture and society. In other words, if the word is used differently, then the statement is no longer true. For instance, in America, the 'first floor' of a building is the one at ground level, whereas in the UK, it is the one *above* the 'ground floor'. Words change meaning in this way all the time. Thus, relations of ideas, far from representing an absolute certainty, merely show that terms have equivalent meaning when we use them in the same way.[92] Thus, *a priori* knowledge, far from telling us interesting and absolutely certain things about the world, would seem to merely provide us with a list of 'tautologies'.[93]

Innate Ideas

In the third Meditation, you may recall, Descartes classified the contents of his mind according to the origin of each type of idea. Having done this he discovers that, contrary to what he first thought, some ideas do not seem to come through the senses, but seem, rather, to be already present within the mind itself. He calls these ideas *innate* (meaning 'inborn' or 'present from birth'), and they form a very important part of his argument.

Firstly, they allow him to argue that the most certain knowledge is completely distinct from the information that we receive through the senses. So, even where we understand something physical – as in the wax example – the principles which are understood (mathematical, geometrical, etc.) concern *a priori* knowledge (i.e. that which is before or independent of experience).

Secondly, they allow him to differentiate between the realm of the physical (*res extensa*), and the realm of the mental (*res cogitans*). That which can be conceived of independently of experience is therefore separate from it. Thus, if I can conceive of myself as existing separately from my body, then I am not (essentially) my body.

Thirdly, they help prove the existence of God (and thereby help guarantee his whole system of argument). Since an infinite thing (the idea of God) cannot come from either a finite thing (me or some other less than perfect source), or nothing, then in order for the idea to exist, God must exist also (this is, in effect, the trademark argument).

The full range of innate ideas would therefore include:[94]

1. The idea of God.
2. Basic mathematical concepts.
3. The idea of myself as a 'thinking thing'.
4. The fundamental truths of logic.

If these ideas were not innate, we would be reliant to some extent on the evidence of the senses – which, as Descartes has already argued, are not to be wholly trusted, and the potential falsity of which can only be guarded against by reference to such *a priori* principles. Furthermore, rationalists argue, to consider some of these ideas as originating from experience would mean that we might be wrong about them. But how could we be wrong about '2 + 2 = 4'? Furthermore, what experience could possibly prove that I was wrong? Could I one day come across a situation in which '2 + 2 = 5'? No, the rationalist argues, such ideas are unchanging truths which allow us to make sense of the world, and so cannot be something which we *learn from* the world.

It is tempting here to interpret Descartes, as Hobbes did, as saying that innate ideas must always be present to the mind. And yet, there are times when we are not aware of them (such as in sleep and unconsciousness). However, Descartes replies that we are not born 'knowing' all these things, but rather that when these ideas are understood by the mind, they are not *created* by experience, but only *suggested* by it. Thus, rather than the idea being 'always present to us', it is merely always available to us.[95]

For the rationalist, a physicist working on a theory that accounts for the behaviour of certain particles is dealing primarily with rational ideas. He forms the theory in his mind, and then applies it to the thing he is studying to see if it can explain and predict its behaviour. Similarly, Plato thought that experience helped to jog our memory for us to 'remember' innate ideas. So, in a famous example, a young boy is guided to 'remember' certain mathematical truths by responding to questions which 'bring out' his innate knowledge.[96]

The empiricist challenge to this was to argue, as Locke does, that the contents of the mind come either from outside (through the senses), or by the mind acting upon itself (considering the ideas it has received). Therefore, Locke concludes, 'we have nothing in our minds, which did not come in, one of these two ways'.[97] So, for empiricists such as Locke, the mind was a *tabula rasa* or 'blank slate' which became written on by experience. This is not to say, however, that Locke did not believe that such principles were certain, but only that their certainty did not rest on them being innate.[98] One of Locke's criticisms is that if such ideas did in fact exist, then we should all be aware of them, and yet '*children* and *idiots*, have not the least apprehension or thought of them'.[99] As we have already seen, however, Descartes is not saying that innate ideas force themselves on our attention, but rather that when we do understand them, they are not *learnt from*, but rather *suggested by*, experience.

> Furthermore, in a reply to Gassendi,[100] Descartes admits the key role of sense experience in *uncovering* these ideas. Gassendi objects that those born blind do not have an idea of colour, nor do those born deaf have an idea of sound. However, after pointing out that there is no possible way that Gassendi can know this, he admits that if blind and deaf people do lack these respective ideas, it is only because they have not had the required experience to *bring out* the ideas. Furthermore, he points out that simply because someone lacks an idea (or is not aware of it) doesn't mean that it doesn't in fact exist (that is, even though the blind person cannot *see* the world, the visually perceptible world still exists).

However, the criticisms of Locke and Gassendi do highlight an important point: if we need experience in some way in order to know these ideas, then why not consider experience as wholly responsible for them? In other words, for Locke, Gassendi, and other empiricists, the only way we could prove that there were innate ideas is that if young children, the uneducated, the blind, the deaf, etc., already possessed them (otherwise, they could be said to spring from experience).

This said, the debate is not a particularly easy one to resolve. Immanuel Kant attempted to do so by claiming that both empiricism and rationalism embodied important ideas, and that the way to resolve the problem was to combine aspects of their different approaches. So, for instance, Kant believed that what the rationalists thought of as innate ideas could in fact be understood in terms of limits or *categories* of human understanding. Thus, as modern science now knows, an apple is not 'really' red, but only appears so to our human visual apparatus (i.e. our eyes and brain), and would be different – for instance – to a dog or a cat. As for colour, so for shape, space, number, and awareness of time. Kant therefore argued that such faculties of perception and understanding allow us to produce what he called 'synthetic' judgements – i.e. statements that tell us something new, such as 'that ball is red', or 'all bachelors can cook'. In such cases, something new has been added (producing a *synthesis* of one thing and another – e.g. 'red' and 'ball'). Such statements may be contrasted with what Kant called *analytic* statements, which merely show how an idea can be *analysed*. For instance, 'the ball is round', or 'all bachelors are unmarried men', are examples where we are talking about ideas (roundness, being unmarried) which are essential to the concepts being considered (ball, bachelor), and therefore merely represent an *analysis* of it (and do not add anything new).

Kant's solution to the problem of how we come to know mathematical principles – which the empiricists had difficulty in explaining – was to say that they were *both* a priori *and* gave us new knowledge (were *synthetic*). So, whilst mathematical principles are *a priori* (inasmuch as we have not formed them through experience), and necessary (i.e. they could not be any other way, and are certain), the knowledge which we achieve of them and through them is *synthetic* (in that we need experience to understand them, and they give us something new). Kant's scheme therefore presents us with a new category of 'synthetic *a priori*' knowledge, which would not have existed for either the empiricists or rationalists.[101]

In summary, while few modern philosophers would wish to sign up to the same list of ideas that Descartes considered innate, the argument is not a dead one. In terms of what is learnt or acquired (*nurture*) and what is present in us because of our constitution (*nature*), the debate still continues – though these days it is much more likely to centre on issues in brain science or psychology.

Foundationalism and the Cartesian Circle

Foundationalism

Descartes's picture of how knowledge may be guaranteed is known as *foundationalism,* in that an absolutely certain thing acts as a *foundation* on which to build subsequent knowledge. In this way, the picture resembles somewhat an upside-down pyramid.

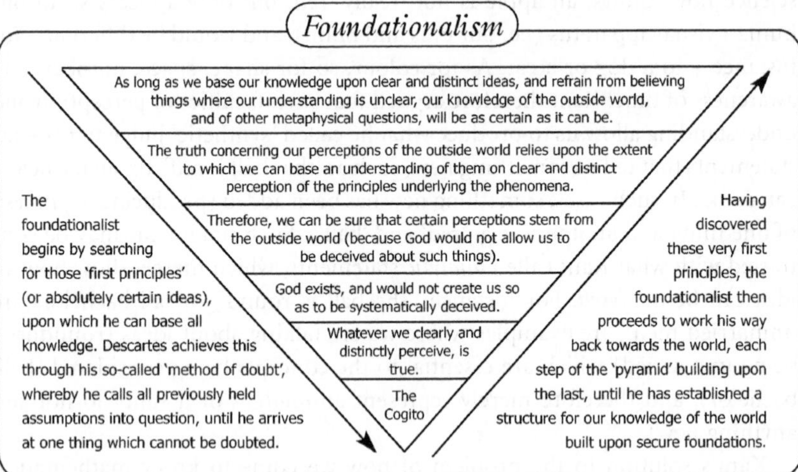

As you can see, the bottommost part acts as a support (foundation) for the more numerous upper parts. Descartes is therefore saying, 'once we know at least one thing with absolute certainty, we can use it to support those things of which we are less certain'. In Descartes's case, the bottommost foundation is therefore the *Cogito* ('I think, therefore I am'), and the upper parts refer to different assumptions about the nature of ourselves, the world, and individual things in the world. But is all well in the world of upside-down pyramids (philosophically speaking)?

The Cartesian Circle

One of the most famous criticisms of Descartes's philosophy, first pointed out by Arnauld,[102] concerns the way in which he uses the existence of God, and the notion of clear and distinct ideas, to support one another. An outline of the problem goes something like this:

SCEPTIC: How do I know that I exist?
DESCARTES: Because I clearly and distinctly perceive that I do.
SCEPTIC: How do I know that I am not deceived in this?
DESCARTES: Because God exists and is not a deceiver.
SCEPTIC: How do I know that God exists?
DESCARTES: Because I clearly and distinctly perceive that He does.
SCEPTIC: But how do I know that clear and distinct perceptions are true?
DESCARTES: Because God exists and is not a deceiver.
SCEPTIC: Hang on . . . !?

As you can see, it would seem that Descartes needs God to prove that our most certain knowledge (which is based on clearly and distinctly perceiving things) is in fact true. The reason for this, if you recall, is that if God did not exist then it might be possible that some evil demon might deceive Descartes (or else, simply, that Descartes is just an imperfect being with an imperfect understanding). However, if God exists, then the possibility of our being systematically deceived is also removed (God, after all, being good, would not create us so as to be constantly mistaken about things).

However, here comes the problem: like any certain truth, God's existence seems to rely on our clearly and distinctly perceiving that He exists (for instance, that the ontological argument is true). But isn't Descartes relying on God to guarantee the trustworthiness of clear and distinct perceptions? It would appear then that Descartes's argument is circular: clear and distinct perceptions need God, God needs clear and distinct perceptions, which in turn need God, and so on. This problem is therefore known as the *Cartesian Circle*.[103]

Descartes's reply to this objection is that there is in fact no circularity involved. The reason for this, he argues, is that at the time when we clearly and distinctly consider something to be true, we 'have assumed a conviction so strong that nothing can remove it'.[104] Now, if we then go on to ask whether such a conviction can in fact be false, we are asking a separate question (i.e. whether God exists or is a deceiver). However, since we cannot doubt His existence or goodness, we must in fact reject this doubt.

Descartes's answer here, however, does not seem convincing, because he does not seem to grasp the full force of the objection. It seems that he is trying to argue that if we deal with each question separately (the existence of God, the notion of clear and distinct ideas), then there is no problem, as our absolute

(*Continued*)

conviction *at the time* is what guarantees things. However, since it is this very notion that he is seeking to guarantee, it would seem that his reply fails. For, even if he is not using God to guarantee this immediate and direct apprehension that something is true, then he must either just trust it, or admit that it is possible that we are (at least sometimes) mistaken – but then the whole edifice of the *Meditations* falls apart – doesn't it?

Perhaps this would not be such a problem for Descartes if he was not seeking to guarantee every aspect of his knowledge. In searching for something absolutely certain, he has to find an answer to the question, 'And how do you know *that*?' His answer – 'because it is clearly and distinctly true' – simply *begs the question* (as philosophers say). In other words, we are still left with the same unanswered question. But how *could* we answer the question in a way that does not beg another one? As we have seen, Descartes's attempt seems to lead us in a circle, but it could just as easily result in what is called an *infinite regress*. If, instead of answering the question, 'How do I know that clear and distinct perceptions are trustworthy?' with, 'because God is not a deceiver', he had invoked some other reason (such as, 'because I get a funny feeling in my toes'), and then when questioned about how he was sure of *that*, provided some other reason, and so on, then we would say that there is no one thing which guarantees the certainty of the knowledge in question, but a potentially infinite string of reasons (because we could always ask, 'And how do you know *that*?'). So, if this string never comes to an end, we can never find a safe place on which to base our knowledge.

The problem, then, for Descartes, is not just that his method seems to result in a circularity, but that even if it did not, we are always left looking for a reason

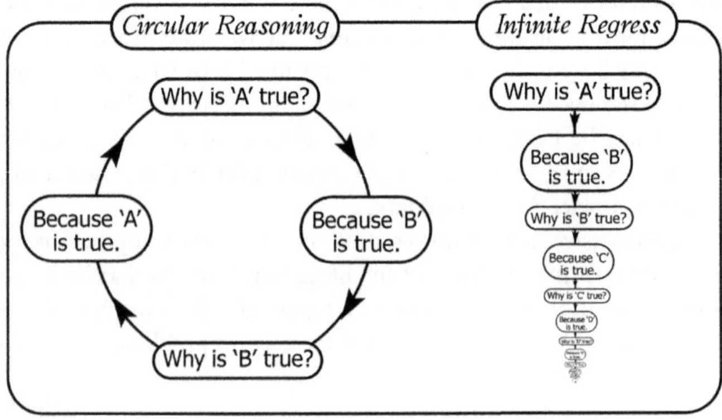

why something is true. Of course, we could just try to stop this process by simply answering, 'Well, it just *is* true' – and in a way, this is what Descartes does. Clear and distinct perceptions, he says, just *are true*. We are innately equipped to perceive the truth of ideas directly. However, this presents us with a bigger problem than circularity or infinite regress, because all we are left with is Descartes's assertion that something *just is true*. But if that is the case, what is to stop anyone asserting things which they 'strongly believe' or 'clearly and distinctly perceive' to be true? This would leave us with a type of *fideism*, or the assertion that knowledge rests ultimately on a belief or faith that something is true.

Alternatives to Foundationalism

Perhaps the problem here, then, is with foundationalism itself. In seeking to find something immune to doubt, we either go round in circles, regress infinitely, or make a dogmatic assertion (e.g. 'I just *believe* it to be true'). For the non-foundationalist, however, there are a number of other options:

1. Perhaps the answer lies in abandoning this idea of absolute certainty. We might adopt a *pragmatist* attitude to knowledge (as did the American philosophers associated with this idea, William James, John Dewey, and C. S. Peirce). Thus, instead of insisting on absolute certainty, we might just say, 'Well, our knowledge *seems* to be working for us. I seem eventually to find out when I've been wrong in the past, and I can do all sorts of useful things with my knowledge – like invent toasters, and computers, and hamster wheels. Who needs absolute certainty?'[105]
2. Instead of thinking in terms of building, we might adopt a different structure for our model of knowledge, and look for different relationships between the things that we hold to be true. For instance, *coherence theory* argues that all our knowledge forms a coherent whole, and that anything that doesn't fit the picture, i.e. is *incoherent*, is therefore false. This is a bit like asking a number of witnesses to an accident, 'What happened?' in order to find out what the most likely course of events was.[106]
3. We might argue that there are limits and restrictions which language imposes upon us, and that while it makes sense to ask certain questions (to which an answer can be found by investigation, although not with absolute certainty), other questions represent 'invalid moves' in the 'language game'. Some things, therefore, while they may not be certain in Descartes's sense, it may not make sense to question. So, while it makes

> sense, from a religious perspective, to ask, 'Who made the world?', it would not make sense to ask, 'Who made God?', because the term 'God' implies a being that has always existed.[107]

It may be argued, however, that there are flaws in all of these approaches: what works is not necessarily what is true, even if we never find out that it isn't; even if most people (or perceptions) agree, it is not necessarily the case that this is an indication of truth (most people used to believe in a flat Earth, remember?); who or what decides what it is valid or invalid to question, or which 'game' we are playing? However, following this thread leads us far away from an introduction to Descartes and the *Meditations*, so there I must leave you.[108]

Notes

Introduction

1 A. N. Whitehead, *Process and Reality*, corrected edition (New York: Free Press, 1978), p. 39. The Greek philosopher Plato (c. 428–347 BC) is often thought of as the first great Western philosopher.

2 It may surprise you to find out that Descartes made a number of contributions to scientific thought, most notably in mathematics through the notion of 'Cartesian coordinates' (as they are now called).

3 See the 'Dedication' to the *Meditations*.

Chapter 1 Background

1 The biographical details in this section are taken from Tom Sorell's Introduction in *A Discourse on Method, Meditations and Principles* (London: Everyman Classics, 1986), pp. vii–xxii, the Introduction in F. E. Sutcliffe's translation, *'Discourse on Method' and 'The Meditations'* (London: Penguin Classics, 1968), pp. 7–11, and Stephen Gaukroger's excellent *Descartes: An Intellectual Biography* (Oxford: Oxford University Press, 1995).

2 Whilst the *Meditations* was originally published in Latin, it was later translated into French, perhaps in an attempt to make the work accessible to people who were not scholars or academics, or who had not had the benefit of an extensive education.

3 *A Discourse on Method, Meditations and Principles* (London: Everyman, 1986), 'Introduction', pp. xvi–xvii. Galileo had been in trouble with the Church since 1616, when he first expressed support for the Copernican system. However, with the publication of the *Dialogue Concerning the Two Chief Systems of the World* in 1632, the Church felt that he had overstepped the mark.

4 The Inquisition, founded in 1542, was a 'combination of law court and board of censors' (*A Discourse on Method, Meditations and Principles* (London: Everyman, 1986), 'Introduction', p. xvi), and it was a much-feared institution, having power to imprison, torture, and put to death those whose ideas or actions threatened the authority of the Church.
5 *A Discourse on Method, Meditations and Principles,* 'Introduction', p. xvii. However, after seeing that this work did not get him into any trouble, his later works were all published under his own name.
6 *The Concise Routledge Encyclopaedia of Philosophy* (London: Routledge, 2000), entry on 'Medieval Philosophy', pp. 552–60.
7 Galileo was not the only eminent name to suffer at the hands of the Inquisition, another notable injustice being the burning at the stake of the heretical Italian philosopher, Giordano Bruno, in 1600.
8 A musket ball is a small, round type of bullet used in musket rifles (which were commonly used between the sixteenth and eighteenth centuries in Europe).
9 Peter Tallack (ed.), *The Science Book* (London: Weidenfeld & Nicolson, 2001), p. 60. (There is obviously more to gravity and free fall than I have room to discuss here, but I trust that the explanation I have given will do for my purpose.) There is some disagreement not only about whether this experiment actually took place, but also concerning the extent to which Galileo used practical experiments at all in arriving at his conclusion. It is safe to say, however, that his scientific practice was probably more theoretical than some scientific textbooks would admit, and that many of his conclusions were based on argument and supposition. However, I've kept the Pisa experiment as my example simply because it illustrates the problem more strikingly than any other example (and also because I don't think it has yet been proven that it certainly *didn't* happen!).

Chapter 2 Explanation and Summary of Main Arguments

1 René Descartes, *Meditations* (London: Penguin Books, 1968), p. 102 (beginning of Meditation II). Note: all quotations from the *Meditations* will come from this translation of the text by F. E. Sutcliffe (unless otherwise stated) because it has a more contemporary tone than the Everyman edition (translated by John Veitch), and also because it is the one used by the AQA examining board when setting extracts for exams. The exception to this is where the Sutcliffe edition does not include certain material (such as the 'Dedication' and 'Preface to the Reader'), in which case I will quote from the Veitch translation. Accordingly, from this point on, *Meditations* will refer to the Sutcliffe translation (unless otherwise stated).
2 *Meditations*, p. 122 (Mediation III).
3 *Meditations* (London: Everyman, 1986), p. 73 ('Preface to the Reader').
4 *Meditations*, p. 96 (Meditation I).

5 *Meditations*, p. 95.
6 *Meditations*, p. 95.
7 For instance, the *Matrix* trilogy of films, the novels of Philip K. Dick, and so on – see the 'Bibliography and Suggested Reading' for more examples.
8 *Meditations*, p. 96.
9 See the section on 'Rationalism vs. Empiricism' in Chapter 3.
10 *Meditations*, p. 98.
11 Examples of the appearance of this scenario in books and films can be found in the bibliography.
12 *Meditations*, p. 99.
13 While the *Meditations* might seem as if it is being thought out afresh as it goes along, this is something of an illusion, the key ideas in Descartes's philosophy having been in place for a good number of years beforehand (even before the *Discourse on Method*, which itself contains much of the same material as the *Meditations*). See n. 21 below.
14 *Meditations*, p. 100.
15 *Meditations*, p. 100.
16 *Meditations*, p. 100.
17 *Meditations*, p. 102 (Meditation II).
18 *Meditations*, p. 103.
19 Like Plato, Descartes seemed to hold that mind and soul were the same thing. However, there are other views – to be found in certain strands of Buddhism, Hindu philosophy, or even Neoplatonism – where a distinction is made between (for instance) the vehicle of continued existence after death, and the intellectual faculty. In some cases, the latter is seen as but one aspect of the former. However, for Descartes, the main activity of the soul would seem to be thinking – a claim that, as we shall see, raises some awkward questions later on.
20 *Meditations*, p. 103.
21 The *Discourse on Method*, or, to give it its full and much grander title, *Discourse on the Method of Rightly Conducting the Reason, and Seeking Truth in the Sciences*, was first published in 1637, four years before the *Meditations*. In Part IV, however, we have what is essentially the structure of the *Meditations* itself. It is here that we first come across the *Cogito* in its most famous form:

> while I thus wished to think that all was false, it was absolutely necessary that I, who thus thought, should be somewhat; and as I observed that this truth, *I think, hence I am*, was so certain and of such evidence, that no ground of doubt, however extravagant, could be alleged by the sceptics capable of shaking it, I concluded that I might, without scruple, accept it as the first principle of the philosophy of which I was in search. (*A Discourse on Method*, (London: Everyman, 1986), pp. 26–7)

We also find the phrase appearing in *The Principles of Philosophy*, published in 1644: 'but we cannot in the same way suppose that we are not while we doubt of the truth of these things; for there is a repugnance in conceiving that what thinks does not exist at the very time when it thinks. Accordingly, the knowledge, *I think, therefore I am*, is the first and most certain that occurs to one who philosophises orderly' (*Principles of Philosophy* (London: Everyman, 1986), p. 167, 'Part I: of the Principles of Human Knowledge', section VII).

22 *Meditations*, p. 105.

23 *Meditations*, p. 107.

24 Talking about 'internal' and 'external' worlds is a sort of occupational habit in philosophy of mind (a bit like 'tennis elbow', 'hitchhiker's thumb', or 'librarian's frown'). In one sense, of course, it is just a way of speaking. However, some philosophers (e.g. Gilbert Ryle) have argued that such language can mislead us into assuming that there is a special 'place' where a separate, non-physical thing called the 'mind' exists, and traces this sort of 'error' back to Descartes himself.

25 *Meditations*, p. 108.

26 *Meditations*, p. 108.

27 *Meditations*, p. 109.

28 It should be noted here that by 'imagination', Descartes is referring generally to the ability to form mental images. Therefore, the term includes not only – as we would normally use it today – the process of creating some 'imaginary' mental picture (as an artist might envision a fantastic animal), but also the process whereby we form mental images of the real world (i.e. the formation of mental representations of physical things).

29 *Meditations*, p. 112.

30 It is technically more correct to term Baruch Spinoza (1632–77) a *pantheist* (someone who believes that God and the universe are one and the same thing). This isn't to say that he didn't believe in some sort of divine consciousness, but merely that God was not separate from His creation (whereas most Christians believe that He is 'transcendent' or separate from creation). To a certain extent, the philosophies of both Spinoza and Gottfried Wilhelm Leibniz (1646–1716) can be seen as responding to, and disagreeing with, aspects of Descartes's philosophy. The philosophy of Bishop George Berkeley (1685–1753) is more commonly known as *idealism* and embodies the idea that matter – as we usually think of it – does not in fact exist, but is rather a mental construction consisting of certain non-physical attributes.

31 In discussion of God, I have generally capitalized the personal pronoun (i.e. He, His, Him, Himself), and also assumed that He is male. This is partly out of respect for religious believers, partly because we are dealing with Christianity (and it is traditional to do so), and partly to make it easier to distinguish between 'he' (Descartes) and 'He' (God).

32 *Meditations*, p. 113.

33 *Meditations*, p. 113.

34 *Meditations*, p. 113.

35 *The Principles of Philosophy*, in *Descartes: Key Philosophical Writings* (Ware: Wordsworth Editions, 1997), p. 293 (section 45).

36 See *The Principles of Philosophy* in *Descartes: Key Philosophical Writings*, p. 294 (section 46).

37 You may still not be happy – or clear – about this definition, and you are entitled to be. However, I shall critically examine the concepts involved in Chapter 3.

38 To avoid confusion, what Descartes calls *ideas* I shall simply call *images*. I shall use the term 'ideas' in its more common modern sense of 'a thought' (whether it involves images or otherwise).

39 *Meditations*, p. 116. A siren is a creature from Greek mythology somewhat like a mermaid, whose beautiful song was said to lure unwary sailors onto the rocks (you can find them in Homer's *Odyssey*). Hippogryphs have lately come to wider popular attention via J. K. Rowling's Harry Potter books (see especially *Harry Potter and the Prisoner of Azkaban* (London: Bloomsbury, 1999)), but can actually be found in many old myths. They are often represented as a sort of cross between a horse and a griffin (which was itself a cross between a lion and an eagle). The Chimera, also from Greek mythology, was a female, fire-breathing monster with a lion's head, the body of a goat, and a serpent's tail. More generally however – and in the sense in which Descartes uses the word – a chimera is a fearful product of the imagination.

40 This point is actually a debateable one, and I shall return to it later (see the section on 'Certainty and Doubt', in Chapter 3).

41 Of course, an empiricist – such as Locke – would point out that factitious ideas must ultimately be formed from adventitious ideas. So, having the idea of a hippogryph would already consist of being familiar with the ideas of an eagle, a lion, and a horse, respectively, via experience. Descartes would not disagree with this, but would add that we might also generate ideas by combining acquired (adventitious) ideas with innate ones (while the empiricists would consider innate ideas to be merely derived from experience – and so, ultimately, stemming from reflection upon adventitious ideas).

42 It might turn out that unicorns exist – though, we might argue, this cannot amount to it being true that such things would be unicorns, since a myth is not a theory of something's nature or existence (see, for instance, Saul Kripke, *Naming and Necessity* (Cambridge, MA: Harvard University Press, 1980)), while other philosophers disagree. However, we may still argue that factitious ideas can play a part in the search for knowledge (as when we form a hypothetical idea of something which we then test – as in our search for the structure of the atom). However, this use of factitious ideas in a scientific context must be limited by experiment, and I am not suggesting that we could arrive at the structure of the atom by simply daydreaming!

43 At least, this is one interpretation of Plato in light of the 'Myth of Er', which appears at the end of the *Republic*. One can, of course, merely take this story as symbolic (and therefore not to be taken as a literal expression of Plato's beliefs), but it is equally valid, I think, to argue that he did actually hold such beliefs.

44 Definitions are taken from the *Oxford English Reference Dictionary* (Oxford: Oxford University Press, 1996). For more on this topic see the 'Rationalism vs. Empiricism' section in Chapter 3. Both these terms spring from the medieval *Scholastic* tradition of philosophy, in which Descartes would have been schooled, but was largely reacting against. For this reason, he would not have used the terms himself, striving to develop his own philosophical language. However, since the terms are still commonly used in philosophical circles (and courses), I think it helps to try to understand Descartes's project in those terms.

45 *Meditations*, p. 117.

46 *Meditations*, p. 119.

47 *Meditations*, p. 119.

48 Though you can buy extremely high-powered, flesh-cutting water pistols – but mine is just your common or garden, 'get you slightly wet' model.

49 *Meditations*, pp. 123–4.

50 Here, and elsewhere, Descartes seems to equate both imperfection and being finite (limited), and being perfect and infinite (unlimited).

51 *Meditations*, p. 125.

52 *Meditations*, p. 131.

53 *Meditations*, p. 134.

54 *Meditations*, p. 134.

55 *Meditations*, p. 137.

56 This version of the argument is an adaptation by Descartes of one originally put forward by the English theologian, St. Anselm (1033–1109). For more on this, see the section 'The Existence of God' in Chapter 3.

57 *Meditations*, p. 148.

58 'Cartesian' simply means 'of or relating to Descartes'. So, one might say 'Cartesian philosophy', or even 'Cartesian moustache'. 'Cartesian', by the way, is the adjective formed from the Latin version of Descartes's name, 'Cartesius'.

59 It is a peculiar but quite well-documented medical fact that individuals who have had a limb amputated can sometimes still 'feel' it to be there (so, a patient who has just had a leg amputated may still describe an itch in their big toe!). Since medicine considers this to be merely a trick of the mind, such 'limbs' are thought of as 'phantoms' or 'ghosts' of the limb that was once there. Interestingly, this false sensation has been treated in some cases via use of a mirror, whereby, for example, a patient who has had her left arm amputated would hold her right arm against the mirror (so as to create a reflection that would look like her left arm). Then, she would flex the muscles in that limb (e.g. clench her fist), and obviously the reflection would do the same, creating the illusion that her left arm was clenching its fist. However, since the patient obviously has no left arm, the brain is finally made to realize – because there is no sensation of 'clenching' – that the left arm doesn't exist! All this suggests that the body is 'mapped' onto the brain, and that some accidents (such as sudden amputations) leave the map intact (but out of date). Some fascinating examples of this problem can be found in Oliver

Sacks's wonderful book, *The Man Who Mistook His Wife for a Hat* (London: Picador, 1985), Chapter 6, 'Phantoms' (pp. 63–6).

60 *Meditations*, p. 156.
61 *Meditations*, p. 156.
62 I go into these issues in more detail in the section on 'Dualism' in Chapter 3.
63 *Meditations*, p. 159.
64 *Meditations*, p. 159.
65 *Meditations*, p. 158.
66 A similar view was held by such thinkers as John Locke and Galileo.
67 *Meditations*, p. 158.
68 A shortened form of *hydropsy*, but now more commonly known as *edema*.
69 In Descartes's time, the *common sense* was thought to be an additional sense to the main five of touch, taste, sight, smell, and hearing, which combined the information from them so that it is possible to get an overall 'picture'. Since, roughly speaking, this is what the brain does, I have simply used 'brain' instead so as to avoid the modern use of *common sense* to mean 'practical, down-to-earth judgement'.
70 *Meditations*, p. 167.

Chapter 3 Critical Themes

1 *Descartes – Key Philosophical Writings*, from the introduction by Enrique Chávez-Arvizo, pp. xviii–xix.
2 There is some confusion in some quarters as to whether it should be 'skepticism' or 'scepticism'. However, the matter is fairly simple: 'scepticism' is the English spelling, while 'skepticism' is the American one, so you will always find me using the former.
3 See *The Routledge Encyclopaedia of Philosophy* (London: Routledge, 2000), entry on 'Protagoras', p. 721.
4 *Routledge Encyclopaedia of Philosophy*, entry on 'Gorgias', pp. 322–3.
5 *Routledge Encyclopaedia of Philosophy*, entry on 'Sophists', p. 850.
6 *Routledge Encyclopaedia of Philosophy*, entry on 'Pyrrhonism', pp. 727–8.
7 *Routledge Encyclopaedia of Philosophy*, entry on 'Carneades', p. 124.
8 For a brief account of Descartes's motives in publishing – and not publishing – certain works, see John Cottingham, *Descartes* (Oxford: Blackwell, 1986), pp. 12–19.
9 *Descartes: Key Philosophical Writings*, 'Objections and Replies', pp. 191–2.
10 'Objections and Replies', p. 192.
11 'Objections and Replies', p. 192.
12 Plato, *The Republic*, translated by Desmond Lee (London: Penguin, 1987), Bk X, section 2(d), p. 370.
13 'Objections and Replies', p. 193.

14 Sir James Jeans, *Physics and Philosophy* (London: Cambridge University Press, 1942), p. 90.
15 See D. Z. Phillips, *Introducing Philosophy: The Challenge of Scepticism* (Oxford: Blackwell, 1996), Chapter 1.
16 'Objections and Replies', p. 194.
17 Ludwig Wittgenstein, *On Certainty*, quoted in Ray Monk's *Wittgenstein: The Duty of Genius* (London: Vintage Books, 1991), p. 578.
18 I have had a small number of lucid dreams to date, and the first thing I always do is to try to fly. My thought process goes something like this: 'That doesn't make sense. . . . ? I know! I must be dreaming! Fly! Fly! Ooh, look, I'm in the clouds! That cloud looks like a camel . . .' and I'm back in the dream (I challenge anyone to do better). Interestingly, though, Descartes experienced a number of lucid and visionary dreams when a young man, and their content influenced him in becoming a philosopher (See Cottingham, *Descartes*, 'Appendix: Descartes Dreams', pp. 161–4).
19 *Meditations*, p. 168.
20 *Meditations*, p. 168.
21 'Objections and Replies', p. 195.
22 'Objections and Replies', p. 195.
23 See the sections 'The Existence of God' and 'Foundationalism and the Cartesian Circle' respectively.
24 'Objections and Replies', p. 197.
25 'Objections and Replies', pp. 197–8.
26 A. J. Ayer, *Language, Truth and Logic* (London: Penguin, 1946), p. 31. This point is also well made (before Ayer) by the German philosopher Friedrich Nietzsche – see *Beyond Good and Evil* (London: Penguin, 1990), Part One, Section 17 (p. 47).
27 The best examples of this are, of course, animated cartoons, in which not only insects and animals, but anything from cars, to toasters, to mountains, can possess human-like personalities. I blame Disney.
28 David Hume was not necessarily arguing that the self does not exist, but merely that when we go in search of it, all we discover are our own thoughts and perceptions. This has become known as the 'bundle theory of self', in that since the owner of these experiences cannot him/herself be an experience (we cannot find one experience which is 'the self'), therefore the self must consist in the total 'bundle' of these experiences, which must be connected together in some way. Hume then looked for some feature that would unite these different experiences. However, this becomes an issue for the personal identity debate (what makes a person *the same* person), and I do not have room to go into it here. See K. T. Maslin's *An Introduction to the Philosophy of Mind* (Cambridge: Polity Press, 2001), pp. 269–71 (which, incidentally, is currently the best available text for A Level students on this topic).
29 'Objections and Replies', pp. 198–200.

30 'Objections and Replies', p. 198.
31 See Chapter 3, n. 93.
32 See Descartes's reply to Hobbes and Gassendi, 'Objections and Replies', pp. 198–202.
33 'Objections and Replies', p. 196, and pp. 197–8.
34 'Objections and Replies', pp. 197–8.
35 'Objections and Replies', p. 196.
36 See Chapter 2, n. 35.
37 As you may guess, I am no physicist. I have given a very simple – though hopefully not incorrect – account of gravity here as a simple illustration. Also, please note: this is not Descartes's definition of gravity, nor is it an example used by him (though he was critical of the contemporary scholastic account and was as interested as many other scientists of the time in arriving at a more correct theory). Sir Isaac Newton, the first to formulate a theory of gravity close to our modern understanding, did not publish his theory until 1687 (thirty-seven years after Descartes's death).
38 *Meditations*, p. 146 (fifth Meditation).
39 There is a big debate in philosophy of maths as to the true nature of numbers. Plato thought that they were real 'things' of which we sought knowledge, whereas many empiricist philosophers would prefer to view them as mere *conventions* (i.e. just a certain way of categorizing and describing the world). There are problems with both views, but most modern philosophers of mathematics tend to steer clear of anything that treats maths as a form of mysticism (which, arguably, Platonism does).
40 It may seem to some that I have contradicted myself here. Earlier, in discussing Descartes's views on maths, I said that the rules of maths *could not* be treated as a game. However, here I am implying that they *can*. What I really mean, however, is that although we may not be able arbitrarily to change the rules of maths (as we might change the rules of any made-up game), there may be a sense in which the rules are not absolutely fixed. For instance, if aliens ever do land, we may discover that they have a different mathematics from ours. However, we may just find that their maths has different rules from ours (they play a different 'game'). In this sense, learning what '3' means is like learning what moves can and cannot be made in a game (rather than realizing some eternal and unchangeable truth). This is actually a rather complicated subject and represents an ongoing debate in modern philosophy.
41 For more on this, see the later section on 'Foundationalism and the Cartesian Circle'.
42 We have already discussed Descartes's response to this problem above when considering how he knows that he is a thinking thing without a chain of reasoning (syllogism). See 'Objections and Replies', pp. 196 and 197–8.
43 Quoted in John Cottingham, *The Rationalists* (Oxford: Oxford University Press, 1988), p. 32.

44 Derek Gjertsen, *Science and Philosophy: Past and Present* (London: Penguin, 1989), pp. 122–3. This and other examples in this section are taken from Gjertsen's discussions of Descartes's method at pp. 102–4 ('Cartesian hypothesis'), and later at pp. 120–3 ('Cartesian deductivism').
45 Gjertsen, *Science and Philosophy*, p. 103.
46 Gjertsen, *Science and Philosophy*, p. 103.
47 Actually, Descartes thought that there were three types of substance in the world: mind, matter, and God. However, since nothing technically can exist without God, Descartes only uses the word 'substance' to mean those things which (relative to God) rely on nothing else for their own existence.
48 See John Cottingham, *A History of Western Philosophy: 4 – The Rationalists* (Oxford: Oxford University Press, 1988), pp. 75ff.
49 This aspect of Spinoza's thought lends itself easily to mysticism, as my mind (and your mind) are, theoretically, all part of the same substance (which we might call 'God').
50 Leibniz's system is meant to address a problematic consequence of Descartes's view of mental substance pointed out by Spinoza (i.e. that it cannot differentiate between individual mental substances). I shall deal with this objection and solution later on in this chapter.
51 See John Heil's excellent *The Philosophy of Mind: A Contemporary Introduction* (London: Routledge, 1998), pp. 23–6.
52 'Objections and Replies', pp. 246–9.
53 'Objections and Replies', p. 247.
54 *Meditations*, p. 159.
55 The *Passions of the Soul*, I. 31.
56 That is, roughly speaking, all animals possessing a spine and skull (cranium) in which the brain resides.
57 'Objections and Replies', p. 248.
58 'Objections and Replies', pp. 248–9.
59 For a very detailed, scholarly treatment of these arguments, see Gary Hatfield, *Routledge Philosophy Guidebook to Descartes and the 'Meditations'* (London: Routledge, 2003), pp. 245–58.
60 'Objections and Replies', pp. 228–38.
61 'Objections and Replies', pp. 243–5.
62 'Objections and Replies', pp. 245–6.
63 See Rita Carter, *Mapping the Mind* (London: Weidenfeld & Nicolson, 1998), pp. 42–53. The example I have used is a typical one, though the details are somewhat more complicated than I have had space to go into here.
64 Actually, the relationship between hands, eyes, and hemispheres is more involved than this. The left hand is related to the right hemisphere, and vice versa; however, regarding the eyes, the left side of each eye's visual field is related to the right hemisphere, and vice versa. However, when it comes to ears, there is no opposite relation (the left ear is related to the left hemisphere).

65 Cottingham, *The Rationalists*, p. 118.
66 'Objections and Replies', pp. 238–9.
67 'Objections and Replies', pp. 202–4.
68 While, in the main, Western science favours a materialist view, there are controversial cases where patients in hospital have reported having been aware during brain surgery (where, at the time, brain monitoring reported no activity).
69 Gilbert Ryle, *The Concept of Mind* (London: Penguin, 1949), p. 17. The whole first chapter, 'Descartes's Myth', is worth reading as a sort of 'antidote' to Descartes. Ryle is often called a 'behaviourist' in that he tries to account for the mind in terms of actual or possible behaviour, though this may not be wholly fair or true.
70 *Routledge Encyclopaedia of Philosophy*, entry on 'Malebranche, Nicolas (1638–1715)', p. 521.
71 See Cottingham, *The Rationalists*, pp. 84ff.
72 Cottingham, *The Rationalists*, p. 103.
73 Cottingham, *The Rationalists*, pp. 101–7.
74 Which I shall not go into here. For good, readable accounts of these see Heil, *The Philosophy of Mind*, Chapter 2: 'Descartes's Legacy', pp. 13–48, and Stephen Priest's – also excellent – *Theories of the Mind* (London: Penguin, 1991).
75 This view is held by – for example – such philosophers as John Searle and David Chalmers (see the bibliography for books by these and others). See also K. T. Maslin's *An Introduction to the Philosophy of Mind*, Chapter 6: 'Non-Reductive Monism', pp. 162–86. Maslin also has good sections on the other theories.
76 See the section 'Foundationalism and the Cartesian Circle' in this chapter.
77 'Objections and Replies', pp. 206–8.
78 'Objections and Replies', pp. 206 and 209.
79 See John Hick (ed.), *The Existence of God* (New York: Macmillan Publishing, 1964), pp. 39ff.
80 'Objections and Replies', pp. 219–20.
81 Hume's argument is actually directed at the teleological or design argument, but the same objection is relevant here also. See his *Dialogues Concerning Natural Religion*, Parts V and VIII.
82 'Objections and Replies', p. 212.
83 See, for instance, his essay, *The Will to Believe*.
84 Of course, even if God exists, it may not be possible to prove that He does (a position held by the Danish philosopher Søren Kierkegaard (1813–55), among others).
85 It should be noted, however, that not all rationalists believe in innate ideas.
86 For more on this distinction – and its limitations – see Cottingham, *The Rationalists*, pp. 1–4.
87 Cottingham, *The Rationalists*, pp. 7–10.
88 Locke held a view similar to this inasmuch as, although he agreed with the rationalists that there were necessary connections between certain events, he did not believe that we could know them. See Cottingham, *The Rationalists*, pp. 9–10.

89 David Hume, *An Enquiry Concerning Human Understanding*, 3rd edn. (Oxford: Oxford University Press, 1975), p. 78.
90 For more on Hume's views, see *An Enquiry Concerning Human Understanding*, Section VII, 'Of the Idea of Necessary Connexion', pp. 60–79.
91 *An Enquiry Concerning Human Understanding*, Section IV, 'Sceptical Doubts Concerning the Operations of the Understanding', pp. 25–39. Hume's division of ideas into 'matters of fact' and 'relations of ideas' is commonly known as 'Hume's fork'.
92 Obviously, one of the problem areas for this sort of understanding of *a priori* knowledge is mathematics, and I shall discuss this in the next section on innate ideas.
93 Tautologies are statements which are true by virtue of their 'logical form'. That is, when I have a statement such as 'all bachelors are unmarried men', we can say that both the terms 'bachelor' and 'unmarried man' mean the same thing. So, another way of saying that this type of statement is true is to say that 'terms which mean the same thing have the same meaning' (or 'A = A') – which is obvious! Hence, the word 'tautology' is also used sometimes to refer to occasions when people express themselves badly – for instance, 'The food was adequate enough to feed 5 people'. 'Adequate' and 'enough' mean the same thing, so we should either say 'The food was adequate . . .' or 'The food was enough. . . .' Using both words is 'tautologous'!
94 Cottingham, *Rationalists*, pp. 70–4.
95 'Objections and Replies', p. 210.
96 The example of the slave boy can be found in Plato's dialogue *Meno*.
97 John Locke, *An Essay Concerning Human Understanding* (London: Penguin, 1997), Book II, Chapter I, section 5, p. 110.
98 C. R. Morris, *Locke, Berkeley, Hume* (Oxford: Clarendon Press, 1931), pp. 22–4. Locke, Berkeley, and Hume all proposed alternative accounts of how the ideas which the rationalists called innate could both be thought of as certain, and yet stem from experience. However, I won't go into those accounts here, but only consider the criticisms they imply.
99 John Locke, *An Essay Concerning Human Understanding*, Book I, Chapter II, section 5, p. 60.
100 'Objections and Replies', p. 211.
101 This is rather a simplification of Kant, but his views are difficult to summarize briefly. For a really good guide to his ideas, however – even if you only read the introduction! – seek out Sebastian Gardner's *The Routledge Philosophy Guidebook to Kant and the 'Critique of Pure Reason'* (London: Routledge, 1999).
102 'Objections and Replies', pp. 223–4.
103 Because the objection is usually associated with Arnauld, it is also sometimes called 'Arnauld's circle' (Cottingham, *The Rationalists*, p. 49).
104 *Objections and Replies*, p. 225.
105 *The Routledge Encyclopaedia of Philosophy*, entry on 'Pragmatism', pp. 704–5.

106 Robert Audi, *Epistemology: A Contemporary Introduction to the Theory of Knowledge* (London: Routledge, 1998), pp. 188ff.

107 I am thinking here primarily of Wittgenstein's approach to philosophy, which concludes that because we must learn language and concepts in order to communicate with, describe, or understand the world and its inhabitants, it may not make sense to question the rules of that game *while also trying to play it*. However, this is a brief (and possibly misleading) summary of Wittgenstein's philosophy, so for those interested in finding out more, you might check out Ray Monk's *How to Read Wittgenstein* (London: Granta, 2005), or even the wonderful biography of Wittgenstein by the same author (see *Wittgenstein: The Duty of Genius* (London: Vintage Books, 1991)). However, even the extremely brave should steer clear of Wittgenstein's works until they have some idea of what his basic approach entails (on which Monk's book is excellent). After this, the best place to start is probably Wittgenstein's *Philosophical Investigations*, ed. and trans. G. E. M. Anscombe and R. Rhees (London: Blackwell, 1953).

108 This subject is properly part of the area of theory of knowledge (or 'epistemology', to give it its proper title), which deals with the definition of knowledge, how we can be certain, etc.

Appendix A: Overview of the *Meditations*

Below follows a brief summary of the main arguments in the *Meditations*. It is meant to aid you in establishing the order and significance of each step.

<table>
<tr><th>Meditation</th><th>Arguments</th><th>Subject</th></tr>
<tr><td rowspan="7">First</td><td>Descartes asks the question, ‘Of what can I be absolutely certain?’</td><td rowspan="3">The Argument from Illusion</td></tr>
<tr><td>He rejects the evidence of the senses, arguing that they too often prove unreliable.</td></tr>
<tr><td>However, he stops short of doubting everything he experiences (he would have to be mad to do that).</td></tr>
<tr><td>He considers whether or not he may be dreaming, and is forced to accept that he cannot be sure (for we may dream that we are awake).</td><td rowspan="3">The Argument from Dreaming</td></tr>
<tr><td>However, the images must come from somewhere. So, just as artists make up imaginary creatures (such as centaurs) using real ideas (man, horse), so even our false ideas must ultimately be made up of simpler ideas which correspond to reality in some way.</td></tr>
<tr><td>He concludes that sciences such as mathematics and geometry are the most trustworthy, as they do not rely on experience (but a priori knowledge).</td></tr>
<tr><td>He rejects God as a possible source of our own errors and tendency to be mistaken. But what if there were a ’malicious demon’ whose sole purpose it is to deceive us?</td><td>Malicious Demon</td></tr>
</table>

<table>
<tr><th>Meditation</th><th>Arguments</th><th>Subject</th></tr>
<tr><td rowspan="8">Second</td><td>The senses are untrustworthy, but who or what is responsible for these perceptions I have of the 'outside' world?</td><td rowspan="3">Malicious Demon/ Cogito</td></tr>
<tr><td>Either it is God (who would not deceive us), a malicious demon, or ourselves.</td></tr>
<tr><td>In the worst-case scenario – that there is a malicious demon – we can still be sure of at least one thing: even if we are deceived, we must exist in order to be deceived. At last! Something certain!</td></tr>
<tr><td>Descartes rejects mere descriptions of what he is – 'man', 'rational animal', etc. – as unsatisfactory. But what then is he?</td><td rowspan="3">Mind and Body Dualism (res cogitans and res extensa)</td></tr>
<tr><td>He decides that the one thing common to all his actions is thought: therefore, he is a 'thinking thing' (Latin: res cogitans).</td></tr>
<tr><td>This thinking thing is separate and distinct from his body, so there must also exist another non-thinking, 'extended substance' (Latin: res extensa).</td></tr>
<tr><td>In examining a piece of wax, he concludes that there is nothing about it – its size, shape, smell – that is not potentially subject to change.</td><td rowspan="2">The Wax Argument</td></tr>
<tr><td>However, since the behaviour of the wax can be understood and predicted, its real nature therefore lies in our intellectual understanding of it.</td></tr>
</table>

Meditation	Arguments	Subject
Third	Division of thoughts into images, desires, and judgements, only the latter of which can be false.	**Division of Thoughts and Relation to the Outside World**
	Classification of judgements as adventitious (originating from outside himself), factitious (created by himself), and innate (present from birth).	
	Rejects the natural tendency to believe that adventitious ideas have an objective source (i.e. the physical world), because such 'natural beliefs' can be mistaken. Therefore, he must find a better reason for believing that his perceptions of the outside world are in fact trustworthy.	
	Concludes that certain ideas (such as mathematical and logical ones) seem more clear and distinct than others (such as heat and cold), which are relative or uncertain.	**Clear and Distinct Ideas**
	The most clear and distinct idea seems to be that of God.	
	Concludes that all things must have as much reality in their cause as in their effect, and that God is the most real (clear and distinct) idea.	**The Trademark Argument**
	Rejects the idea that he himself is in some way responsible for the idea of God, and proposes that therefore the idea must have been placed in him almost like some trademark left by a craftsman (God) on his creation (Descartes). Therefore, He (God) exists.	

Meditation	Arguments	Subject
Fourth	Rejects God as the possible source of human error (He is not a deceiver, because He is all-good).	**The Cause of Error**
	Rejects the idea that his own faculty of judgement is responsible, because that was created by God. 'Will' is perfect and unlimited (we can always say 'no'), whilst 'understanding', though finite, is – for all we know – adequate for the purposes God intended.	
	Concludes that it is the misuse of the will (for which we are solely responsible) which is the cause of error, in that we do not stop ourselves passing judgement on those things we don't know enough about (and feel 'indifferent' about).	

<table>
<tr><th>Meditation</th><th>Arguments</th><th>Subject</th></tr>
<tr><td rowspan="2">Fifth</td><td>Concludes that because we have the idea of a perfect being (God), He must exist, because not to exist would mean that He is less perfect.</td><td rowspan="2">The Ontological Argument</td></tr>
<tr><td>Rejects three objections to this argument on the grounds that we necessarily have the idea of a perfect being, who, by definition, must exist.</td></tr>
</table>

<table>
<tr><th>Meditation</th><th>Arguments</th><th>Subject</th></tr>
<tr><td rowspan="5">Sixth</td><td>Distinguishes between understanding (conception) and imagination, associating the first more closely with pure thought, and the second with representations of the external world, and sensations relating to the body and the senses.</td><td rowspan="3">Mind and Body</td></tr>
<tr><td>The most certain things can be clearly and distinctly conceived of, but the least certain can only be imagined. Therefore, the further we get from clear and distinct perceptions, the more likely we are to fall into error.</td></tr>
<tr><td>Mind is more closely related to the body than the pilot is to his ship, because we feel the body's hurts immediately. However, both are potentially separate from one another, and we can conceive of the mind as existing without the body.</td></tr>
<tr><td>Rejecting God and himself as possible sources of sense impressions, he accepts the idea that they originate outside himself as the most likely possibility.</td><td rowspan="2">Certainty and the Outside World</td></tr>
<tr><td>Concludes that, although our senses and natural assumptions commonly lead us into error, they can provide useful information if we use our reason to keep them in check.</td></tr>
</table>

Appendix B: Selected Summaries of *Objections and Replies*

The following table is compiled from the selection of the *Objections and Replies* in *Descartes – Key Philosophical Writings* (Wake: Wordsworth Editions, 1997), pp. 191–260. The arguments summarized below, however, are themselves only a selection of *that* selection, and represent only those discussed in this book, or those which I considered interesting (I have left out some of the more obscure or complicated objections). I have grouped the arguments by Meditation and 'Topic', following the Wordsworth edition (to which 'Page(s)' refers). The surnames of the objectors are listed underneath the number of the 'Set' of objections (for more on these, see the Glossary). The arguments are sometimes complex and difficult to summarize, so I have paraphrased quite freely, occasionally adding my own comments (between square brackets) to round out the answer. For serious study, there is really no substitute for the original, so curious students should hunt out the actual text.

Meditation I				
Topic	**Set**	**Objection**	**Reply**	**Page(s)**
Method of Doubt	7 (Bourdin)	Is it really necessary to doubt all of our former beliefs?	Yes, in order to weed out the 'bad apples' (our false beliefs) from the 'good apples' (the true ones).	191
	7 (Bourdin)	Why should we concentrate on skepticism (when nothing really is exempt from doubt)?	We need to identify the strongest arguments in order to find the cure for them (just as a doctor studies a disease).	192
Argument from the Senses/ Illusion	6 (Mersenne)	Understanding does not correct the 'bent-stick' error, it is touch.	But what makes you trust the sense of touch more than sight? You need a reason to do this (provided by the understanding).	193
	5 (Gassendi)	The mere existence of errors shouldn't make us distrust *all* judgements.	Yes, but it is possible to be wrong about even the things you hold to be most true – you need a reason to trust your judgement, otherwise all you have is prejudice.	193–4
Dreaming Argument	3 (Hobbes)	Can't we dream that our experiences seem 'coherent'? Are only religious believers entitled to be certain of things?	Yes, we may be mistaken that we are awake, but not that we *have been* dreaming (we know for sure when we wake up). However, we can only be *absolutely certain* of this if we also believe in God as a non-deceiver (atheists are therefore doomed to uncertainty).	194–5

Meditation II				
Topic	**Set**	**Objection**	**Reply**	**Page(s)**
Cogito	2 (Mersenne)	You cannot clearly and distinctly know that you are a 'thinking thing' without first proving that God exists (in order to guarantee clear and distinct perceptions) – which, at this stage, hasn't yet happened.	The knowledge that I am a thinking thing is not arrived at deductively (via syllogism), but is a sort of 'primitive knowledge' which is immediately apparent. God is only necessary to guarantee syllogistic reasoning.	196
	5 (Gassendi)	Doesn't our reason tell us that what acts also exists? Why use only thinking as proof of existence?	We cannot say, 'I walk, therefore I am', because physical actions may be illusory (as in dreams), whereas mental actions are even present in the dream state.	197
	6 (Mersenne)	You cannot say 'I think, therefore I am' without first knowing what is meant by 'thinking' and 'existence' – which, at this point, you do not. But how will you ever *get* to know these things? It seems impossible.	There is an 'internal cognition' that always precedes reflection. So, in order to ask the question, 'What is thinking?' I must base my reflection on something which is apparent to me, some sort of internal experience. It is this, therefore, that forms the basis of the *Cogito*, and not a string of reasoning based on prior definitions of 'thinking' and 'existence'.	197–8

Nature of the Mind	3 (Hobbes)	It is all very well to say 'I am a thing which thinks', and that therefore I exist, but why should this thing be an incorporeal mind? For, you should not confuse a thing's essence with its activities. For instance, we could not say, 'I walk, therefore I am *the walking*'. However, that is what you are doing, because you are saying, 'I think, therefore I am *the thinking* (i.e. therefore an incorporeal substance)'.	In saying 'I am a thinking thing', the terms 'mind', 'spirit', 'intellect', and 'reason' are not meant to describe faculties, but are alternative names for the same substance: the thinking thing. So, while 'walking' can only be an action, 'thinking' can describe the action, the faculty, or the thing which acts. This is not to say, however, that the action and the thing which acts are the same, but merely that at times I have used the word to mean the action, and at other times to describe the thing which acts.	198–9
Nature of the Mind	3 (Hobbes)	You seem to be lapsing back into the old Scholastic way of talking: the Will wills, the Vision sees, the Understanding understands, etc., making it out as if these actions were things in themselves, distinct from their subject (me).	I *am* distinct from my thought, but only in the sense that a thing is distinct from its activities. But when I ask what exists apart from my thought, I am not saying 'I am thinking', but merely asking, 'What is there which is part of "me" which is not thought?' [In this sense, my body is inessential to 'me' – I can imagine myself without it – therefore only thinking is essential to 'me'.]	200

Meditation II (*Continued*)

Topic	Set	Objection	Reply	Page(s)
Nature of the Mind	5 (Gassendi)	We are not so much interested that you are a 'thinking thing', but rather as to *what* you are. This, you do not tell us, and it would have been of greater interest to find out what the nature of the 'substance' is that 'you' are made of (in a similar way that science can tell us of the makeup of the physical body).	I have given a clear idea of what I am, and if you are looking for anything more, then you have a confused idea of what is possible. A substance may be understood by its attributes [as the wax was understood by the variance of its shape, size, texture, etc.], and the more we know something's attributes, the better we know the substance. Therefore, since the mind is the one thing through which we know *all* attributes, then it is best known of all, because we can see its working in the understanding of the different aspects of things.	200–2
Animal Souls	4 (Arnauld)	If we can prove that we have a soul because mental substance is separable and distinct from the body, then what about animals? They must have some sort of soul to account for the types of conscious behaviour that they sometimes display, but how then are these souls different from human ones?	Animals share with human beings the machine-like operations of the body by which instinct guides us. As we know, a great deal of our own behaviour is accomplished by the body's own instincts (walking, breathing, the beating of the heart, etc.), and the soul does not control them directly, but by the same 'animal spirits' which direct the behaviour of animals). However, this similarity aside, we must not be fooled into believing that animals too possess some sort of rational soul [which belongs only to humans].	202–4

The Wax	3 (Hobbes)	[If imagination cannot grant us direct knowledge of things as they really are, then] you need to show how your method of conceiving with the mind [or clearly and distinctly perceiving] is different from imagination (which you do not). Perhaps, in fact, all our reasoning does is link words together according to conventional (but arbitrary) meanings [instead of the direct grasping of innate ideas, as you think it is]. Therefore, reason will actually depend on names, which in turn rely on imagination, which in turn is stimulated by physical bodies outside of us [as empiricism thinks. So, for instance, that triangles have 3 sides is just a convention (it could be different), and not an innate idea.]	I have clearly shown that imagination and conception are two different ways of approaching the world, and that only the latter can give us a true picture. Furthermore, it must be the case that reason is based not just on names, but on what those names stand for [the ideas], for how else could a German and a Frenchman reason about the same thing? But you have fallen into your own trap, for you talk about words 'signifying' something – but what, if not an idea?	204–5

Meditation III				
Topic	**Set**	**Objection**	**Reply**	**Page(s)**
Trademark Argument	3 (Hobbes)	Since God is inconceivable, how could we possess an image or idea of Him?	Of course, while we can have no accurate image of God, we can nonetheless possess a direct perception of Him, just as we can have ideas of things without images (such as acts of will and desires).	206
	2 (Mersenne)	How do you know that you have not received the idea of God from your upbringing (e.g. books, conversation)? Natives of different countries do not possess it. The idea you have [of physical perfection] could have come from the physical world, and you could easily construct an idea which did not actually exist in reality.	Even if I did receive the idea of God from books, family, etc., where did *they* get it from? The idea of God that I have is not an image, but an act of the understanding alone. It is similar to the way in which we understand the infinite when we realize that you can go on counting forever. There is no infinite number, as such, but we understand the idea of infinity from this process – so do we understand the idea of God. Finally, God is only unthinkable in the sense that we cannot adequately conceive of Him; however, this is different from the type of idea which merely lets us know that He exists. [We might say that we cannot conceive of infinity, or a complex pattern, but we can still experience it and so know it exists.]	206–8

Trademark Argument	3 (Hobbes)	If there is no idea of God, then the argument collapses. Furthermore, I do not have an image of the soul, but a chain of reasoning from the idea that *something* must be responsible for moving my body.	There is an idea of God, but not an image, just as there is with the soul. [All our ideas do not come from sense impressions, but we may arrive at them through reason – so, just because we do not have images of God and the soul, this does not mean that they do not exist.]	209
	3 (Hobbes)	We can have many conflicting ideas of a thing (e.g. the sun), and it is our reason which finds out the truth, not any one of the ideas themselves.	What you call 'ideas', I call 'images', and when you talk of arriving at the truth through reason, I talk of understanding the true idea. [So, we cannot agree while we disagree in this way (about how words have meaning).]	209
Innateness	3 (Hobbes)	If innate ideas exist, they must always be present to us – and yet we sleep and are sometimes unconscious, and so they cannot exist.	By 'innate' I merely mean that which is imprinted in us from birth. Therefore, the idea is not 'always with us', but rather 'always available to us' (we have the ability to realize it).	210

Meditation III (*Continued*)				
Topic	**Set**	**Objection**	**Reply**	**Page(s)**
Innateness	3 (Hobbes)	When I look at the attributes of God, I find that they could in fact stem from ideas of external objects.	This cannot be the case, for there is nothing in God which is found in external objects. However, by observing our own mental processes, we may eventually arrive at an idea of the intellectual activity of God. Similarly, reflecting on the world, we realize that the fact that it exists means that it must have been created by God. [Thus, by reflection on many things, we may arrive at the idea of God.]	210–11
	5 (Gassendi)	Those born blind had no idea of colour. Those born deaf, no idea of sound. Isn't this because their senses are closed, and so those ideas could not be formed? [Therefore, such ideas are not innate, but are learnt.]	We do not really know whether the blind have an idea of colour. But besides, even if they do not have those ideas, this is not to say that those ideas do not exist. For, we might as well argue that the world does not exist because a blind person doesn't see it, as that these ideas do not exist. [Note: Descartes seems to be conceding here that experience plays a role in bringing forth innate ideas, though not in forming them.]	211
Reality and its Degrees	3 (Hobbes)	When you say 'more reality', does this make sense? Can you have 'more' or 'less' reality? [Isn't something just 'real' or 'not real'?]	A substance [e.g. rock] has more reality than its modes [e.g. its texture or colour], and an infinite substance [e. g. God] has more reality than a finite one [e.g. man]. [Note: Reality for Descartes therefore seems to relate to how independent, clearly and distinctly perceivable, unchangeable, etc., it is.]	212

Meditation IV				
Topic	**Set**	**Objection**	**Reply**	**Page(s)**
On Error	3 (Hobbes)	Error is not [as you say] a defect, for we need the faculty of reason (or at least, imagination) in order to fall into error. Therefore, when you say that error is due to a misuse of the faculties of understanding and will, you contradict yourself. Finally, you also assume that we have freewill – but how can we if God has preordained everything?	Firstly, error is indeed due to a failure to exert our will in line with our understanding, and is therefore a defect in the sense that we have not used them properly [not that they are defective, and so I do not contradict myself]. Secondly, concerning freewill, everyone experiences this and knows it to be true. How this fits in with divine predestination we do not know, yet anyone reflecting on his own freedom to act can see that to will and to be free are the same thing.	214
	3 (Hobbes)	Your phrase, 'great mental illumination', is a bit vague – and besides, anyone who just believes something strongly can be said to have the same 'illumination' – even though he might be wrong. Secondly, knowing and believing have nothing to do with the will, because whether we see something as true or believable is not up to us. Therefore, you have not proved that the misuse of free will is responsible for error.	The term is fine as long as it explains things – which it does. All I mean by it is, 'to clearly understand something' – though, perhaps, not everyone who thinks he has it in fact does. However, it is still different from just having a strong opinion. Secondly, we cannot say that we have no say in what we believe or hold to be true, because to will is to give your backing to something, and we cannot say that we both 'do' and 'do not' hold something to be true. [That is, we have a choice, and if what was true forced itself on us against our will, then that would make no sense, for we could not decide either to believe or not to believe it.]	215

Meditation V				
Topic	**Set**	**Objection**	**Reply**	**Page(s)**
Ontological Argument	1 (Caterus)	Even though you can have a clear idea of a supreme being, and that such a being would necessarily include existence as part of its essence, this does not mean that such a being does actually exist.	We can think of the *possible* existence of any number of things, but we cannot say that God *possibly* exists [because it would be a defect]. Add to this that God is different from all other things in that, He can exist by His own power, and that such a being must exist, then we can see that the idea we have of Him is not a mere fiction.	218
	5 (Gassendi)	You seem to be treating 'existence' as a property of an idea, whereas in fact it is more correct to talk of whether the thing which that idea represents truly exists. In comparing triangles and God, the comparison should be between properties of those ideas (e.g. 'having 3 angles', and 'omnipotence'), then whether those ideas exist. Therefore, your argument does not seem to prove that God necessarily exists.	By 'property' I mean 'that which can be predicated of a thing', which surely existence can. Furthermore, 'necessary existence' can only be said to belong to God, and so it must form part of His essence [in order to differentiate Him from things which 'just happen' to exist]. God *is* His own existence, whereas a triangle is not (its existence and essence can be separated). However, I grant that existence would also be a higher perfection in ordinary things (since not to exist would be less perfect).	219–20

Cartesian Circle	4 (Arnauld)	Isn't there a circular reasoning involved in needing God to guarantee clear and distinct perception, but also needing to clearly and distinctly perceive that God exists?	We know God exists, because we have valid proofs for His existence [which we clearly and distinctly perceive to be true]. However, when we question whether it is possible for us to clearly and distinctly perceive things, it is enough to remember that God exists and is not a deceiver. [Note: Perhaps Descartes's point here is that God guarantees that we can build a chain of reasoning using clear perceptions, not that He guarantees individual perceptions themselves, which are just 'clear and distinct' – though his point still seems somewhat unclear and problematic.]	223–4

Meditation VI				
Topic	**Set**	**Objection**	**Reply**	**Page(s)**
Existence of Material Things	3 (Hobbes)	The evil in deception lies in the bad intention of the liar, and not the lie itself (doctors may tell lies to help a patient, etc.). Therefore, the fact that God is good does not mean that he might not lie to us (or cause us to be mistaken about things). Therefore, it does not follow that material things actually exist [just because they appear to, and God is not a deceiver].	While we are often deceived, we can in no way blame God for this, as he is not a deceiver. [Note: Descartes is therefore seemingly arguing that God would not even tell a 'white lie' for the sake of a greater good, as deception is not in His nature.]	228
Real Distinction between Soul and Body	4 (Arnauld)	I can doubt that I have a body, but this doesn't mean that it doesn't exist. So, though I know my mind is essential to 'me' (I cannot doubt it), it might be that my body is as essential to 'me' as my mind is. [I am aware of myself as a thinking thing, but that does not mean that I am *only* that.] For instance, it is possible to be aware that a triangle possesses certain properties, while also being ignorant that it possesses others *which are equally essential to it*. The argument for treating the two things as distinct is based on the assumption	Even though there may be some aspects of me of which I am unaware, I have a clear enough idea of what is essential to me to be sure that I (the mind) could exist without the body. For, if we can imagine something as not possessing some attribute, then that particular attribute does not form part of its essence. You object, however, that we do not have an adequate idea of mind or body, but we do not need to (nor is it possible to know all the attributes that a thing possesses). Of course, we cannot know what a complete knowledge of a thing would consist of (for that would already be to know	228–38

		that you have clear and complete conceptions of what body and mind are respectively. However, it might be that the mind is just an aspect of the physical body [and therefore reliant upon it]. Therefore, what you need to prove is that the mind actually *is* distinct from the body – which you do not.	the thing completely), so we must have some other means of knowing that our conception of a thing is adequate enough to make a real distinction between it and something else [e.g. between mind and body]. Hence, to know a thing adequately enough we only need to see that the attributes that it possesses are essential to it, and that to take them away would be to strip that thing of its essence (and leave nothing). That a thing possesses certain essential attributes therefore allows me to recognize it as a substance [i.e. a thing which does not rely on anything else for its existence]. In one sense, mind and body *might* [figuratively speaking] be called 'incomplete substances' in that they are both only aspects of a whole, living human being. However, this does not mean that they cannot be considered separately as being complete and distinct – one is not an attribute of the other. The triangle example you use is different in important respects: firstly, the properties a triangle possesses are not separate substances (as body and mind are); secondly, we could not imagine a triangle that does not possess certain properties (whereas, at the very least, we can	

(*Continued*)

Meditation VI (*Continued*)				
Topic	**Set**	**Objection**	**Reply**	**Page(s)**
			imagine a body without a mind); thirdly, certain properties of the triangle (that we are aware of) will be directly linked to other properties (that we are not) – but this is not the case with body and mind [and they can be conceived of completely separately]. Therefore, we can completely and distinctly perceive that body and mind are separate because certain attributes are essential to the mind, and others are inessential (and vice versa with the body).	
Real Distinction between Soul and Body	4 (Arnauld)	Thinking seems to be tied to the physical brain (it is undeveloped in infants, damaged in the insane, etc.).	Just because the state of the physical brain can affect our power of thought does not mean that thought cannot exist without it. However, there would seem to be a close connection between mind and physical substance – which, in fact, is part of the reason why we have trouble in recognizing that they are really distinct substances.	238–9

Real Distinction between Soul and Body	2 (Mersenne)	Remember, you only argued that you could doubt the existence of bodies so that you could prove that you are a thinking thing. So, mightn't it be true that the body (via the brain) is in fact responsible for thought?	I have already, in the second Meditation, discussed this issue [of what thinking is]. However, I did not, at that stage, answer the question fully, but only showed that we know the mind much better than the body, and can conceive of it separately. However, in the sixth Meditation I show that we can conceive of mind and body as separate and distinct substances, and that therefore just as mind possesses no physical properties, so no physical body can think. Furthermore, any one who does not see this is merely constrained by habit, and needs to dwell on the subject more carefully.	239–43

Meditation VI *(Continued)*				
Topic	**Set**	**Objection**	**Reply**	**Page(s)**
Real Distinction between Soul and Body	1 (Caterus)	As Duns Scotus points out, just because we can conceive of things separately does not mean that they can actually *exist* separately.	This is true only of 'incomplete entities' [i.e. those which form part of something else], but the 'real distinction' between mind and body is very different. For instance, I can conceive separately of the shape and the movement of a particular thing, but in reality these cannot exist separately from the thing itself [i.e. they are only 'modes' of that body, and are therefore 'incomplete entities']. However, I *can* conceive of the body completely without it possessing any mental properties, and I *can* conceive of the mind as not possessing any physical properties. I therefore conclude that their distinction is not merely a 'modal distinction' between different properties [as it was with shape and movement], but a 'real distinction' between separate substances.	243–5

Mind–Body Interaction	4 (Arnauld)	Although you distinguish between body and mind, it may be argued that you only do this in an abstract, intellectual way [which does not correspond to reality]. So, for example, in geometry, a line may be defined as 'length without breadth', but in reality, there can exist no such thing. Perhaps, then, the spiritual self is after all joined in some way to the physical body.	I have not argued that man is just a spirit that makes use of a body (as you say), but rather that the mind and body are 'substantially united' (see Meditation VI). However, just because there is a unity of mind and body (as a 'man'), this does not mean that one cannot exist without the other, and that the mind cannot be conceived of separately and distinctly (in this way, it differs from your example from geometry, where pure 'length' is an abstraction, whereas 'mind' is a real, distinct substance).	245–6
	5 (Gassendi)	How do these two distinct substances of mind and matter interact? How can the mind unite with some part of the brain – however small – if it has no physical dimensions at all? How can mind influence the body? [And so on . . .]	Your objections are based on what you imagine to be the difficulties arising from my theories, and not from a criticism of the arguments for dualism itself. Also, your idea of interaction is based on your understanding of how physical things interact, and such an understanding is inappropriate when considering the interaction of mind and body.	246–8

Meditation VI (*Continued*)

Topic	Set	Objection	Reply	Page(s)
Mind–Body Interaction	5 (Gassendi)	If the soul is incorporeal [or 'spiritual'], how does it move the body? Also, how do physical things impress themselves on the mind?	These objections do not affect my main arguments [that body and mind are separate substances], and the problem is not one which it was my intention to deal with in this work. Besides, the whole objection assumes that two such substances *cannot* interact (which has not been proved). Furthermore, there are numerous things which affect a substance (its weight, temperature, etc.) which are not properly part of it, but how do these interact with the substance itself? There is more difference here than between body and mind. [Note: it would be interesting to consider what Descartes's conception of these (to use Aristotle's terms) 'accidental properties' is.]	248–9

Glossary

You will find below definitions for most of the technical philosophical terms used in this book. I have also given explanations of uncommon words (e.g. *dropsy*), and brief accounts of some of the philosophers mentioned. Words which appear in definitions which themselves have a definition have been *italicized*.

Word or Phrase	**Definition**
a posteriori	Referring to knowledge obtained through experience (from the Latin, meaning 'that which comes after').
a priori	Referring to knowledge obtained before or independent of experience (from the Latin, meaning 'that which comes before').
accidental properties	Those properties of a *substance* which are not essential to it, and are therefore subjective or relative to the observer (from *Aristotle*).
adventitious ideas	Those ideas which seem to originate from outside the mind (compare with *innate* and *factitious*).
Aenesidemus	Greek philosopher (1st century BC), founder of a school of philosophy which revived *Pyrrhonism*, a variety of scepticism which taught that absolute certainty is impossible.
affections	Emotions. Among the types of *ideas* identified by Descartes as having no *truth value* (see also *volitions*).
Aristotle	Greek philosopher (384–322 BC), student of *Plato*, and one of the founders of Western philosophy. His philosophy was a main ingredient of *Scholasticism*.
Arnauld, Antoine	French theologian, philosopher, and mathematician (1612–94), who came to share many of Descartes's views. Author of the fourth set of objections.

attributes	(See *Properties*)
Ayer, A. J.	English philosopher (1910–89), for a long time a promoter of *Logical Positivism.*
behaviourism	A general term for the attempt (beginning in psychology and spreading to philosophy) to account for the mind in terms of actual or potential physical behaviour.
Berkeley, Bishop George	Irish philosopher (1685–1753), a proponent of *Idealism*, his own version of which proposed that nothing exists apart from what is perceived (or perceptible) in the mind. Therefore, matter – as we think of it – is an illusion.
Bourdin, Father Pierre	French Jesuit Priest (1595–1653), author of the seventh set of objections (whom Descartes privately considered 'a fool').
'Brains in Vats' Argument	A sceptical argument proposing that, for all we know, we exist as a mere 'brain in vat', fed illusory impulses by an evil scientist (see *deception, argument from*).
Carneades	Greek philosopher (214–129 BC) and radical sceptic. Attacked both religious and philosophical dogma and taught that truth was subjective.
Cartesian	Meaning 'of, or relating to, Descartes', e.g. 'Cartesian Dualism' (from the Latin for Descartes, 'Cartesius').
Cartesian dualism	Descartes's conception of reality as being split into two (dual) substances: mental stuff (*res cogitans*) and physical stuff (*res extensa*). (To be contrasted with *monism*, *pluralism*, and *idealism*.)
Caterus, Johannes	Dutch theologian (1590–1655), and author of the first set of objections. Note: 'Johannes Caterus' is actually a Latinized version of his Dutch name, 'Johan de Kater'.
chiliagon	A thousand-sided geometrical shape.
Chimera	A creature from Greek mythology, which was a female, fire-breathing monster with a lion's head, a goat's body, and a serpent's tail. More generally, however, the term means some fearful but imaginary thing.
clear and distinct ideas	Descartes's criteria for secure knowledge, i.e. that the more clear (forcefully apparent) and distinct (definite and separate from other ideas) an idea is, the more true it is.
Cogito, the	Descartes's argument that whilst he thinks, it must be true that he exists, and therefore he cannot doubt it (for

	to doubt is to think). From the Latin, 'cogito ergo sum', 'I think, therefore I am'.
contingent truths	Knowledge which is based on experience, and which might therefore have been otherwise (e.g. the fact that someone is called 'David' and not 'Charles'). See also *necessity*.
deception, argument from	The argument that we may, for all we know, be the subject of sustained deception as to the true nature of reality, and be unable to know that (hence an argument against the possibility of absolute certainty).
divisibility, argument from	Descartes's argument that, since the body is divisible, and the mind indivisible, they are two separate and distinct substances.
double aspect theory	The theory, most commonly associated with *Spinoza*, that mind and matter are really just two aspects of the same substance.
dreaming argument	The sceptical argument that we cannot tell the difference between waking and dreaming.
dropsy	Short for 'Hydropsy', a condition in which surplus water is retained in the body (now more commonly known as *edema*).
dualism	(See *Cartesian Dualism*)
Duns Scotus	Scottish medieval theologian and philosopher (c. 1266–1308).
edema	(See *dropsy*)
eliminativism	A theory in the philosophy of mind that suggests that our common way of talking about the mind is 'incorrect', and that we should 'eliminate' those terms by 'reducing' them to talk of the working of the physical structures of the brain.
empiricism	The broad philosophical approach that argues that most of our knowledge comes through, or is ultimately based upon, experience.
epistemology (theory of knowledge)	The area of philosophy that looks at the nature of knowledge, how we can guarantee it, what methods best obtain it, etc.
essence	Those properties of a *substance* which are essential to it and define it.
evil/malignant demon argument	Descartes's sceptical argument that supposes that there might exist an evil entity whose sole purpose is to deceive us as to the nature of even the most obvious truths.

extension	The property, which all physical objects have, of possessing length, breadth, and height.
factitious ideas	Descartes's term for those ideas which originate within the mind, but are not innate (e.g. a mermaid).
first principles	The absolutely certain and basic truths upon which all other knowledge can be based.
foundationalism	The approach which suggests that we can build our knowledge upon the 'foundations' of *first principles.*
Galilei, Galileo	Italian philosopher (1564–1642), and one of the founding fathers of modern science. Forced to retract and suppress his heretical ideas under pressure from the Inquisition.
Gassendi, Pierre	French philosopher, scientist, and mathematician (1592–1655). Author of the fifth set of objections.
Gorgias	Greek philosopher and sceptic (c. 483–375 BC). He was a teacher of rhetoric and an important *sophist.*
hippogryph	A creature from myth, represented as a cross between a lion, a horse, and an eagle.
Hobbes, Thomas	English philosopher (1588–1679), author of the great work on political philosophy, 'Leviathan'. Famous for his *materialism.* Author of the 3rd set of objections.
idealism	The philosophical doctrine that everything that we experience is of a mental nature, or even – in its extreme form – that nothing exists apart from ideas (or spirit) – hence a form of *monism.* (See entry on *Berkeley.*)
ideas (images)	In Descartes's usage, 'ideas' refer to mental images. However, I have used it in its common sense, and used the term 'images' to refer to the latter.
identity theory	The *materialist* theory of mind which suggests that mind and brain are actually the same thing (e.g. identical), so that, in fact, the mind is just the physical brain.
illusion, argument from	(See *senses, argument from the*)
imagination	In Descartes's usage, the faculty of producing images (not just imaginary, but as mental representations of the world through the senses).
indifference	Descartes's idea that, to avoid error, we must cultivate a habit of viewing uncertain questions with *indifference* (or calmness of mind), and only agreeing to those things when sufficiently 'compelled' by reason.

innate ideas	Those ideas which are accessible to the mind from birth (and do not stem from experience).
intermingling thesis	Descartes's picture of the mind–body relation, whereby the body is said to 'intermingle' in some way with the mind.
judgements	Statements which can be either true or false.
logical positivism	A philosophical movement, beginning in Vienna in the early twentieth century, which tried to reduce all knowledge to logical truths and that which could be conclusively proven through experience.
Malebranche, Nicolas	French *rationalist* philosopher (1638–1715), influenced by Descartes, famous for his doctrine of *occasionalism*, which argued that God acts as the link between the two substances of dualism (mind and matter).
Mersenne, Friar Marin	French theologian, philosopher, and mathematician (1588–1648). Author of the second and sixth set of objections.
materialism	The philosophical/scientific doctrine that everything that exists in the world is made up of physical particles (to be contrasted with *dualism* and *idealism*).
method of doubt	Descartes's method for arriving at truth by initially doubting everything until those things beyond doubt become apparent.
mind–body dualism	(see *Cartesian dualism*)
monism	The philosophical view that reality consists of only one *substance* (to be contrasted with *dualism* and *pluralism*).
myriagon	A ten-thousand-sided geometric shape.
nativism	The theory that certain concepts and beliefs are innate. Also, in modern terms, the idea that certain ideas and mental capacities stem from the inherent organization of our brains.
natural light	The natural powers of reason.
natural teachings	Those things which, without reflection, we are inclined to believe at first.
necessity	The *rationalist* notion that some truths cannot have been otherwise (e.g. 'every effect must have a cause'). This may be contrasted with *contingent truths*, or things that might have been otherwise (e.g. that a certain building exists).

occasionalism	(see *Malebranche*)
omnibenevolence	Supreme goodness (a traditional property of God).
omnipotence	Being all-powerful (a traditional property of God).
omnipresence	Being everywhere at the same time (a traditional property of God).
omniscience	Being all-knowing (a traditional property of God).
ontological argument	Descartes's argument for the existence of God, based on the assertion that a perfect being must necessarily exist (for not to exist would represent an imperfection).
Plato	Greek philosopher (c. 427–c. 347 BC), often thought of as the founder of Western philosophy. Held, in common with Descartes, a number of *rationalist* views, notably sharing a distrust of the senses, and a belief that true knowledge was founded on innate ideas.
pluralism	The philosophical position that argues that the world is made up of many substances (to be contrasted with *monism* and *dualism*).
premise	A preliminary statement or assumption that forms part of a reasoned argument (see *syllogism*).
primary qualities	Those properties that belong to a *substance* that are not subjective or relative (such as its physical dimensions).
properties	Those qualities possessed by a *substance* (e.g. a 'red' dog, a 'perfect' circle).
Protagoras of Abdera	Greek philosopher and sceptic (c. 481–c. 411 BC), generally included among the *sophists*.
Pyrrho of Elis	Greek philosopher (c.360–c.270 BC), usually credited as being the first sceptic, taught that knowledge was impossible. *Aenesidemus* later founder *Pyrrhonism*, a school of philosophy based on Pyrrho's ideas.
Pyrrhonism	(See *Pyrrho of Elis*)
rationalism	The philosophical approach that argues that reason is the foundation and source of all our knowledge.
res cogitans	(See *Cartesian dualism*)
res extensa	(See *Cartesian dualism*)
Ryle, Gilbert	English philosopher (1900–76), advocated a type of *behaviourism*. Famous for his criticism of Descartes's view of mind, describing it as 'the doctrine of the ghost in the machine'.

scepticism (or *skepticism*)	The general philosophical approach that argues against the possibility of acquiring certainty, or even denies the existence of truth.
scholasticism	The traditional philosophical approach combining the teachings of *Aristotle* and Christian doctrine which was widespread in Descartes's time.
secondary qualities	Those properties of a *substance* which are subjective or relative to the observer (such as colour or smell).
self-evident truths	Those truths which are immediately apparent without following a chain of reasoning.
senses, argument from the	The argument that our senses do not provide us with a reliable .guide to the nature of reality, and that we can never trust them.
Socrates	Greek philosopher and tutor to *Plato* (c. 470–399 BC). Appears as a dramatic character in most of Plato's works (his 'dialogues').
sophist	A teacher of (mainly) rhetoric and philosophy, who proposed that we can have no knowledge of truth (even if it exists), and that therefore 'truth' lies in creating the best argument (see *Gorgias*).
substance	The essential nature of a thing or idea; that which has *properties*, but is not one itself.
syllogism	A form of deductive reasoning which, using two *premises*, arrives at a conclusion.
Timon of Phlius	Greek sceptical philosopher (320–230 BC), generally associated with *Sophism*.
trademark argument	One of Descartes's arguments for the existence of God that proposes that we have the idea of God, and it can have come from nowhere else but from God Himself.
truth value	A sentence has truth value if it can either be 'true' or 'false'.
volitions	Desires. Among the types of *ideas* identified by Descartes as having no *truth value* (see also *affections*).
wax argument	Descartes's assertion that all we know about the physical world comes through an intellectual understanding of its *properties*, and not through the senses.

Bibliography and Suggested Reading

The scientist and author, John Gribbin, once wrote that, 'If all the books and articles written for the layman about relativity theory were laid end to end, they'd probably reach from here to the moon' (John Gribbin, *In Search of Schrodinger's Cat* (London: Black Swan Books, 1984), p. xv). Well, Descartes's ideas have been around considerably longer than relativity theory, and the number of commentaries, guides, and introductions must fill a few library shelves. Add to this the number of sections, chapters, and passing references to his philosophy in works dedicated to other subjects, and you have a substantial literature. So, being the kind, thoughtful person that I am, I have compiled a select bibliography for those who want to follow up this book with further reading.

Accordingly, I have listed the books under sections and commented on the accessibility, coverage, and purpose of each one [in square brackets] at the end of each reference. I have developed a key as shorthand for some of the books to indicate whom it is best suited to:

L = Layperson (intelligent beginner – no knowledge)
A = British A-Level student/US Freshman (intermediate – some knowledge)
U = Undergraduate (introduction at university, A-Level synoptic/detailed study)
D = Degree (suited *only* for intensive study at university level)

I have also included details of books, films, etc., that I think utilize or illustrate some of the philosophical issues with which Descartes was concerned.

A word of caution: this is not an exhaustive list, and I am sure there are many good and worthy publications which are not listed here. Therefore, if you come across or know of something that isn't on the list, then it simply means that I've either not come across it, or don't have room to mention it (but it may still be worthy and readable). However, I have also tried to keep the list quite short – just as road directions should be!

Happy hunting!

Editions of Descartes's Works

René Descartes, *'Discourse on Method' and 'The Meditations'*, trans. F. E. Sutcliffe (London: Penguin Books, 1968). [This is the edition which AQA use to set extract questions for the exam, and therefore the edition I have – almost solely – quoted from in this book.]

René Descartes, *Descartes: Key Philosophical Writings*, trans. Elizabeth S. Haldane and G. T. Ross (Ware: Wordsworth Editions Ltd, 1997). [Contains all of Descartes's writings which the moderately serious student is likely to need. I have used it here for some quotations from other works. Also good for Descartes's *Objections and Replies* to critics of the *Meditations*.]

Books on Descartes and the *Meditations*

John Cottingham, *Descartes* (Oxford: Blackwell, 1986). [**AU:** Excellent book by a Cartesian authority. Readable and yet detailed and informative enough to be more than just an introduction. A good book to follow on from this one.]

Gary Hatfield, *Routledge Philosophy Guidebook to Descartes and the 'Meditations'* (London: Routledge, 2003). [**D**: Very scholarly introduction which covers all the arguments in exhaustive and academic detail.]

Descartes in Context, Rationalism, and the Historical Background

Jacob Bronowski and Bruce Mazlish, *The Western Intellectual Tradition* (London: Hutchinson & Co., 1960). [**LU**: Classic account of the development of ideas from the Renaissance to the nineteenth century, linking together developments in society as a whole. Fascinating and readable.]

John Cottingham, *The Rationalists* (A History of Western Philosophy: 4), (Oxford: Oxford University Press, 1988). [**AU**: Detailed, informative, but readable account of Descartes, Spinoza, and Leibniz, and the intellectual background of the times.]

The Philosophy of Mind

Rita Carter, *Mapping the Mind* (London: Weidenfeld & Nicolson, 1998). [**LAU**: Fascinating introduction to the way in which discoveries in brain science and psychology have changed the way we think about the mind. Easily readable and informative – it's even got pictures!]

Rita Carter, *Consciousness* (London: Weidenfeld & Nicholson, 2002). [**AU**: Follow-up to the previous book attempting to combine a scientific with a philosophical approach to the 'hard problem' (that of explaining consciousness). Slightly more challenging than the last, but worth it – and it has pictures too!]

John Heil, *Philosophy of Mind: A Contemporary Introduction* (London: Routledge, 1998). [**AU**: Interesting, clear and well-written account of current issues stemming from Descartes.]

K. T. Maslin, *An Introduction to the Philosophy of Mind* (Cambridge: Polity Press, 2001). [**AU**: Thorough and detailed account of all the major movements in philosophy of mind aimed at A-Level students, but suitable also for undergraduates.]

Stephen Priest, *Theories of the Mind* (London: Penguin, 1991). [**AU**: Very comprehensive and yet readable account of philosophical theories of mind. Well-written and thorough.]

The Philosophy of Religion

John Hick (ed.), *The Existence of God* (New York: Macmillan, 1964). [**AU**: A reader collating presentations of, and responses to, arguments for the existence of God from Plato to A. J. Ayer. Very interesting and useful.]

John Hick, *Philosophy of Religion*, 4th edn. (Englewood Cliffs, NJ: Prentice Hall, 1990). [**AU**: Very readable and informative introduction to the subject, with good coverage of the main themes, arguments, etc., with a mature approach.]

Anne Jordan, Neil Lockyer, and Edwin Tate, *Philosophy of Religion for A-Level* (Cheltenham: Nelson Thornes, 2002). [**LAU**: Excellent introduction to the subject. Ideal for beginners at any level.]

Theory of Knowledge and General Textbooks

Julian Baggini, *Philosophy: Key Themes* (London: Palgrave Macmillan, 2002). [**LAU**: Concise, point-form overview of the key aspects of the themes studied at A-Level.]

Julian Baggini, *Philosophy: Key Texts* (London: Palgrave Macmillan, 2002). [**LAU**: Companion volume to the above, dealing with texts studied at A-Level (including Descartes).]

Peter Cole, *The Theory of Knowledge* (Coventry: Hodder & Stoughton, 2002). [**LAU**: Brief, readable introduction to the subject.]

Jennifer Trusted, *An Introduction to the Philosophy of Knowledge* (London: Macmillan, 1981). [**AU**: Excellent introduction at a mature level, putting the philosophical problems regarding knowledge into historical context in a clear, narrative style.]

Literature and Film

Books about Films

William Irwin (ed.), *Philosophy and the Matrix* (Chicago: Open Court, 2002). [**LAU**: Collection of essays by different authors on philosophical subjects inspired by the first 'Matrix' film (though there have since been more books in this series on the follow-up films). Some challenging essays, but on the whole very readable and interesting. Especially relevant to Descartes given the nature of the films (i.e. a 'deception' scenario).]

Film and Television (there are hundreds of these – below are just a few of my favourites)

eXistenZ. [Virtual-reality-based dreaming scenario.]

Jacob's Ladder. [The dreaming argument.]

The Matrix. [Deception scenario.]

Memento. [Illustrates the sceptical argument concerning the trustworthiness of memory – would 'clear and distinct perceptions' help our hero here?]

The Singing Detective. [The TV series, not the film! Uses the dreaming scenario in a truly creative way in exploring a wide variety of emotional themes.]

Total Recall. [The problem of memory and personal identity.]

The Truman Show. [Deception scenario.]

Literature

Philip K. Dick. [Most of his stories have some philosophical content, and he is especially fond of sceptical illusion/deception scenarios, so the following titles are just a sample.]

Do Androids Dream of Electric Sheep? [There is so much in this book – more than the film (*Blade Runner*), which is not to belittle a wonderful film – ranging through a number of themes in personal identity and the philosophy of mind.]

Ubik [Dream/reality scenario.]

We Can Remember it for you Wholesale. [Short story later filmed as *Total Recall.* Illustrates sceptical arguments concerning memory and personal identity.]

Index

Note: page references in *italics* refer to illustrations and tables.

Printed in the USA/Agawam, MA
July 22, 2020

758609.007